HUMBLE MASTERPIECES

HUMBLE MASTERPIECES
100 EVERYDAY MARVELS OF DESIGN

PAOLA ANTONELLI

Thames & Hudson

First published in the United Kingdom in 2006 by
Thames & Hudson Ltd, 181A High Holborn, London WC1V 7QX

www.thamesandhudson.com

Photographs by Francesco Mosto
Designed by Richard Ljoenes
With additional text and research by Eva Hagberg

British Library Cataloguing-in-Publication Data
A catalogue record for this book is available from the British
Library

ISBN-13: 978-0-500-28603-6

ISBN-10: 0-500-28603-5

Printed and bound in China

To Larry

INTRODUCTION

Everything is designed, one way or another. Some objects are designed well, while others are not; some are designed pretentiously, others unassumingly; some are designed to optimize materials and techniques, while others are wasteful; some are approachable and understandable, others instead trade on their unattainability. Design takes them all in, from chandeliers to pencils, from airplanes to computer screens, from the interior of a theater to the receipt at a department store's checkout. While some objects naturally attract our attention for their extraordinary character and desirability—an eccentric and expensive pair of sneakers, for instance, or a gleaming sports car—many others are so apparently ordinary as to go unnoticed. Every day we use dozens of them, from elastic bands to Band-Aids, erasers, and mascara wands. If they work well, chances are we won't pay them much attention. However, in spite of their modest price and demure presence, some of these things are true masterpieces of the art of design and deserve our unconditional admiration.

Most everyday objects, like paper clips or bubble wrap, speak of the timeless role of craftsmanship, the timeliness of innovation, and the continuous guidance that material culture can provide. They are anonymous designs in that we often do not know the name of the person who drew them up, the way we instead know who signed a leather bag or a chair. They are frequently identified by a brand, like Swingline or Black & Decker. Some of them are of exceptional quality, affordable, and universal. They are so good, we could not imagine living without them. And still, we take them for granted. The moment we decide to become acquainted with them, a whole new universe opens up. Each object comes with a story that begins with its conception and does not end until it is destroyed or recycled, a life cycle whose narrative can be as captivating as a biography. Take the Post-it note, for example. Its genesis is attributed to a "mistake" by a 3M scientist in the 1960s, followed by a serendipitous recovery by a colleague in the 1970s. Legend has it that, in the process of engineering a new permanent glue, the first scientist came up instead with the composition for a glue that could be repositioned several times without losing grip and without damaging the support surface. In other words, a useless flop. Useless, that is, until it became useful to a second scientist, years later. Its application to a yellow note, an attention-claiming reminder that could be stuck to manuscripts, desks, and walls alike, at the time in the early 1980s of the introduction of the first personal computers, was the beginning of a revolution in the way people organize their thoughts. Hypertext on a refrigerator's door, the Post-it shook the world.

If you found this story gripping, wait until you have a chance to learn more about the Bic pen, the fortune cookie, or the transistor. In order to design these apparently banal objects, Nobel prizewinners, French barons, or Japanese landscape designers tinkered with the latest advancements in the technology of thermoplastics or of semiconductors, and sometimes built empires on one single patent. The history of some objects, chopsticks and dice for example, is lost in time and we can still today lose ourselves in the contemplation of their perfect balance between form and function, their sensible and sensitive use of materials, the way they express the ancient culture that generated them. When an object is well designed, to the trained eye it seems to glow from the inside, proud of how well it performs the function it was intended for and of how effortless it makes everything seem. We are all design experts, even if some of us do not know it. When it comes to utilitarian objects, we should simply be able to tell if they're good or bad, much like a steak. Once we learn to recognize patterns of beauty in pragmatic and economic ideas, we will realize that our kitchen drawers, our purses, our car trunks, and our bathroom cabinets are vibrant museums full of masterpieces.

What makes a good design? An object first happens as an idea. In the designer's mind, the idea is perfect, and so is the object. But the journey from idea to model first, and then working prototype, and in the end, product, is long and perilous. Many forces tear away at the initial perfection—the materials and techniques available, to begin with, and then considerations about marketability, safety, ergonomics, and recyclability. . . . A good designer is able to transform these strictures into inspiration for further refinements and in the end will make sure that we do not miss the initial idea. The object is all we need. A good designer is a good listener who uses experience, curiosity, and sympathy to understand and draw ideas from the surrounding world. A good designer makes us think everything is simple, as if new objects were already in the air. It so happens that some successful designs startle a surprise of recognition, an immediate closeness. They cross all individual and national boundaries to speak a universally personal language.

This book is a collection of examples of great and humble design masterpieces. What all these objects have in common is not only that they are all common—at least in the part of the world they are from. They share many more remarkable traits. To begin with, many of them are useful, so useful that they have become necessary. Even when they are not immediately functional, as is the case with some toys like the Slinky or the Rubik's Cube, they have added so much delight to the history of our material culture that they deserve a prominent space in our world. Moreover, all the objects in this book are affordable, at least by an inhabitant of the northern hemisphere earning a median salary, and are understandable—their form efficiently describes their function. Almost all of them are ingenious and innovative in the way they propose a new solution or an altogether new typology of objects, sometimes an opportunity to take advantage of a technical or scientific discovery. Last but not least, all these characteristics make them beautiful.

Many factors determine our critical appreciation of a design object. Among them, usefulness certainly rates high. A good object has to deliver, if not a full-fledged function, then at least an emotion, some information, a hint of a meaning. The way an object is made is also very relevant: the materials, the technique, the way they complement each other in a rounded economy of thought and action, all contribute to the quest for excellence. And then, one can measure the ethical substance of an object, the way it responsibly addresses both a universal audience and a universal need to protect our limited resources. Moreover, an object needs to express the time and culture that generated it. When it comes to utilitarian objects, beauty is an outcome, a perception that derives from their accomplishments. Many of the objects in this book, like the Zippo, the Tetra Brik, or the safety pin, are icons, but being an icon is not enough: they are all well-designed icons. The beauty of great design is that it's both very complex and very simple. Design is a celebration not only of creativity, but also of determination, intelligence, and diversity.

Despite what you've heard, design is not simply problem solving. In some ways, design is a way to give problems a new form, so people can solve them by themselves. Designers don't really have solutions. They just walk along very human paths, trying to make things easier for other human beings. When it comes to new technology, design makes it more palatable, easier to swallow, but it doesn't solve its problems. Design does not provoke revolutions, but when revolutions or major changes happen, design can help the world deal with them and transform them into positive change. The best contemporary objects are those which through their presence express history and contemporaneity; those which manifest with their physical presence the material culture that generated them, while at the same time speaking a global language; those which carry a memory and an intelligence of the future; those which are like great movies in that they both spark a sense of belonging—in the world, in these times of cultural and technical possibilities—while they also manage to carry us to places we have never visited. The best contemporary objects are those which express consciousness by showing the reasons why they were made and the process that led to their making. Contemporary design is vigorous with experimentation and creativity, projected toward a sustainable future, optimistic, honest, and aware.

Design has become part of common language. It is at last recognized by the world as not only a cultural, but also an economic force. Fashion, costume, and business writers invoke it to describe any sort of lifestyle vagary. Yet, now more than ever, design is still a slippery word. It is used internationally in its English form, and in each language it takes on at the very least three different and distinct meanings. In most cases, it is confused with other bordering fields, such as the decorative arts. In abstract terms, design refers to strategy: each time there is a problem to solve, planning is involved; when the problem is bi- or three-dimensional and it implies visual and functional issues, it becomes named "design." But that would be too simple. What about beauty? What about ergonomics? And engineering, recycling, comfort, and safety? Design is much more complex and deep than problem solving. By keeping a wide perspective, nonetheless, design is a logic scheme that can be applied almost universally. However, design as a discipline still suffers from a general lack of understanding both of its deeds and of its possibilities.

One thing is for sure: design has a tremendous impact on everybody's life, and a better understanding of design will work to everybody's advantage. A remarkable consequence of the evolution of retail into a buyer's market—thanks to mega-retailers and the Internet—is a better education and more assertiveness on the part of people everywhere. As a matter of fact, even at its most lyrical, design is intrinsically constructive, hopeful, helpful, and practical. It can do more than please consumers and businesses: it can influence policy and research, and translate technological revolutions into human format, while providing useful feedback from the field about human needs to scientists and politicians. Design can act as a bridge between the abstraction of strategy and the complex details of the real world. Designers are advocating roles that are more and more integral to the evolution of society. Among those in charge of shaping the future of the world, they are the most benign, responsible, and visionary. Just like the masterpieces in this book, designers' humility will change the world.

Karl Elsener, Swiss, 1860–1918
SwissChamp Knife, ca. 1968
Plastic and stainless steel
Manufacturer: Victorinox, Switzerland

Swiss Master Cutler Karl Elsener designed his first knife for the Swiss army as early as 1891 and registered his invention in 1897. He dedicated the name of his company, Victorinox, to his mother, Victoria, and to the type of steel used for the knife's blade, *inoxydable* (stainless) in French. Moreover, he borrowed the Swiss flag, a white cross in a red field, as his company logo. Every Swiss soldier would receive a knife upon entering the army and thus make it known to the whole world—and as a matter of fact, the knife was a hit with the American GIs during World War II. With the passing of time and with the advent of more advanced production techniques, the original Officer's knife branched out in one hundred different models, each named after the specific type of actions its user will presumably accomplish—the Electrician, the Tinker, the Tourist, and the Prince being four of them. The SwissChamp, shown here, is a variation of the classic Champion designed in 1968, which had sixteen blades and attachments that performed twenty-nine different functions. As with all the different knives, the SwissChamp comes with a lifelong guarantee, although the company claims that knives are very seldom returned.

HUMBLE MASTERPIECES   / Spaghetti/Noodles and Pasta

Unknown Designers
Spaghetti/Noodles and Pasta, thirteenth century
Durum wheat

Pasta has existed for many centuries and is a delicious example of great design. The simple mixture of durum wheat flour and water, shaped or extruded by hand or machine, is such a fundamental and strong design idea that it has been able to generate an endless variety of derivative designs. Moreover, it is a timeless design, in that its production tools have been updated across the centuries, but its basic form has remained the same. It is easy to appropriate and adapt to local culture, so that almost every country has its own pasta dishes. And it is a universal success of critic and public.

Like some other examples of great design, pasta does not have one acknowledged inventor. As a matter of fact, the Chinese and Italians are still arguing on noodles' copyright. Though some claim that Marco Polo brought the noodles back with him to Italy from China in the late thirteenth century, pasta already existed in both places long before. Archeologists have found signs of Etruscan pasta dating from the fourth century BC, and the Chinese were making a noodlelike food as early as 3000 BC. The manufacturing process is rather simple and consistent. Italian pasta, in particular, is made by grinding kernels of durum wheat. The semolina is mixed with water until it forms a dough, and the dough is then kneaded to the correct consistency. It is then pushed, or extruded, through a metallic die with holes that determine the final shape. When the extruded pasta reaches the right length, it is cut with sharp blades that rotate beneath the die. Hard to believe it could be so easy, but the best things sometimes are.

Alfred J. Reach, American, 1840–1928
Benjamin Shibe, American, 1833–1922
Baseball, 1870s
This model: Rawlings ROMLB (Official Major League Baseball)
Manufacturer: Rawlings, USA

The history of America's favorite sport is wrapped up in the history of the sport's ball. The very first baseballs were balls of twine or sheepskin wound around a walnut and covered in high-quality horsehide, wound by hand. Albert Spalding (*that* Spalding) used to reminisce that the first baseballs he remembered playing with were made with the socks of brave volunteers.

The first large-scale manufacturers of baseballs were John van Horn of New York and Harvey Rose of Brooklyn, in the 1850s. They made three-ounce balls from a core of melted old rubber wrapped in sheepskin. In 1875, John Giblin patented a ball made of a core of compressed palm leaves surrounded by woolen yarn and covered in rubber. Four months later, Bostonian Samuel Hipkiss patented a ball with a bell inside, thinking it would assist umpires in making more informed calls. For the next forty years, however, the most important innovations came from Alfred J. Reach and Benjamin Shibe, who teamed up as scientist and salesman, designing, manufacturing, and selling baseballs in Philadelphia. Their first baseball was manufactured without seams, a design choice they made thinking it would keep the ball intact for longer. They soon found that it made curveballs nearly impossible and they replaced it with a double-seamed model.

The first mass-production machine was patented in 1876, but it took until 1889 for a machine that could wind yarn to be invented. Reach's son George (incidentally married to Shibe's daughter Mary) received historical credit for introducing the cork-centered baseball in 1911, finding that the resilience of cork was inversely proportional to that of the ball. Another member of the family, Daniel M. Shibe, received the patent for the double seam.

In an interesting turn of design that baseball aficionados find utterly meaningful, the cross section of a baseball—core, woven material, crust—is remarkably similar to that of Earth.

Unknown Designer
Crochet Hook, ca. 1873
This model: Susan Bates crochet hook
Aluminum
Manufacturer: Coats & Clark's, United Kingdom

Crocheting is one of the most ancient ways of creating a flat material surface out of threads, and is believed to have originated before the Common Era, when people connected threads by looping material through slipknots they created, all with only their fingers. The word crochet is derived from the French word *croche*, meaning "hook," and was practiced in the eighteenth century by French nuns, who brought the practice with them when they traveled to Ireland. Crochet became popular among the leisure class ladies of Victorian England, who used it to construct elaborate trimmings for their linens and undergarments, using silk threads in order to create what often resembled the much more expensive and delicate lace of which they were so fond.

The earliest written instructions are from 1840, but there has been a dearth of records, as it was believed that crocheting skills were simply handed down from generation to generation in the manner of oral history, rather than more publicly explained. In Victorian times it was thought that a woman looked most elegant when she was holding her crochet hook in a manner similar to how pencils are held, but current thought is that carpal tunnel syndrome can result from that position, and avid crocheters are advised to hold the hook in their palms instead. In the end it is the simplicity of the hook that leads historians to believe that the knotting method of creating a long chain that can either be turned on itself and looped together or worked in rows to make a solid material is so compelling that the crochet hook is simply acting as an extension of the bent forefinger.

Unknown Designer, Japanese
Chasen, sixteenth century
Bamboo

This beautiful and inexpensive whisk, used in the Japanese tea ceremony to work the bitter *matcha* green tea to a froth, is not only a functional object, but also an essential part of the ritual. Like the other tools and like the ceremony itself, it is meant to convey harmony, serenity, humility, and refinement. The Japanese tea ceremony, first explored by Zen Buddhist monks as an art form in the fourteenth century, was given definition in the sixteenth century by its founder Sen no Rikyū. He set rigid standards not only for the sequence and choreography of the ceremony, but also for the type of materials used in the tools, which range from wood and bamboo to silk and ceramic. His version of the ceremony is still in use today.

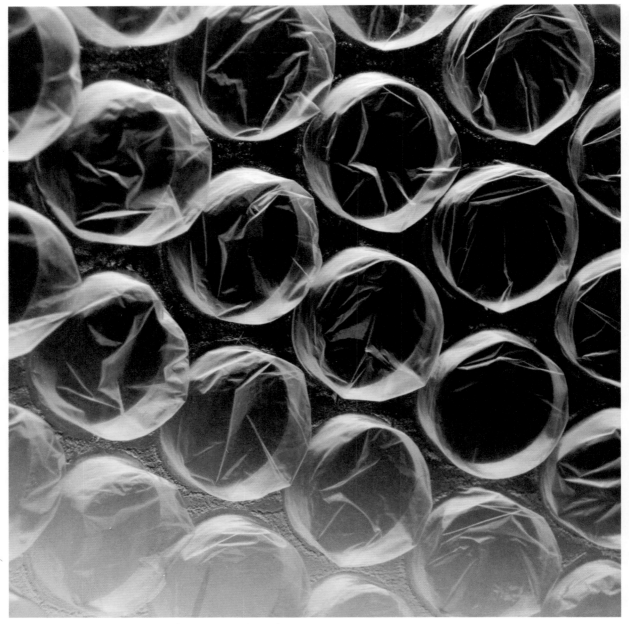

HUMBLE MASTERPIECES   / Bubble Wrap Air Cellular Cushioning

Marc A. Chavannes, Swiss, 1896–1994
Alfred W. Fielding, American, 1917–1994
Bubble Wrap Air Cellular Cushioning, 1960
Polyethylene plastic
Manufacturer: Sealed Air Corporation, USA

In 1957, Marc Chavannes and Alfred Fielding were working in a New Jersey garage on a lukewarm idea for a new type of plastic-backed wallpaper when they happily rerouted the outcome of their research, as well as nine thousand dollars, to develop the ubiquitous cushioning known to the world as bubble wrap that the nervous happily pop and the artistic carefully employ. Bubble wrap is manufactured in a five-part process by laminating together two sheets of polyethylene, one of them formed by suction into bubbles.

The rest is legend and trivia. For instance, we learn that each year Office Depot sells enough bubble wrap to go around the earth twice, and that the product is well known to 80 percent of the world's population. The product has found innumerable applications that stray from its original intention, stress relief, for instance. Bubble Wrap Appreciation Day falls on the last Monday of January.

Swatch, Swiss, established 1983
Swatch Wristwatch, 1983
This model: MoMA Swatch, 2000
Plastic and metal
Manufacturer: Swatch, Switzerland

In the early 1980s, weakened by the competition from a new generation of su-
per-slim and super-cheap Japanese digital watches, two revered Swiss watch
companies on the edge of liquidation, SSIH and ASUAG, and their banks
turned to consultant Nicolas G. Hayek and Hayek Engineering for help. In 1983,
Hayek produced a study that recommended several measures, among them
the merging of the two companies and the development of the Swatch, which
promised to be not only an innovative watch, but also a revolutionary product.
Engineered by Jacques Müller, Ernst Thonke, and Elmar Mock, the cost-sav-
ing Swatch was made of plastic and of only 51 parts, as opposed to the 90 or
even 151 parts of traditional Swiss watches. The movement plate was cast
into the back-cover plate and became a structural rather than decorative element in the design. It is said to have had two precursors: the 1971 Tissot
Astrolon (fifty-two parts only, and plastic wheels, pinions, escapement, case,
and plates, and a low price of fifty dollars) and the 1979 Concord Delirium,
then known as the world's thinnest watch.

   The integrated design of the Swatch ultimately had a huge impact on the
international watch market. The first models, the translucent Jellyfish and
the straightforward GB001, were blank canvas waiting to be adorned by a long
and illustrious queue of artists and transformed into timely collections, affordable limited art series that contributed to the aura of the watch.

Kaspar Faber, German, 1730–1784
Nicolas-Jacques Conté, French, 1755–1805
Lead Pencil, 1761
Graphite and cedar wood
This model manufactured by Faber-Castell, Germany

In 1565, a sticky black substance thought to be lead was found underneath an uprooted tree in the Cumberland hills of the United Kingdom. People began to use it to write erasable marks by inserting it into a rough wooden holder. In the late eighteenth century, the Swedish chemist Karl Wilhelm Scheele identified the material as a crystallized form of carbon and named it graphite after the Greek word *graphein,* which means "to write."

In 1760, a German cabinetmaker, Kaspar Faber, founded his eponymous company near Nuremberg, opening his first pencil shop in 1761. His first pencils were composed of narrow sticks of graphite mixed with sulfur and glued between two pieces of wood. In 1795, French chemist Nicolas Conté developed a superior compound of graphite and clay, which would be fired into a ceramic before being inserted in the wooden case. The innovation allowed not only for a more efficient manufacturing process, but also for a variety of hardness of the graphite soul. The Faber company remained in the family. In 1839, Kaspar's great-grandson Johann Lothar Faber mechanized pencil production by implementing first water and then steam power, and came out ahead of the branding trend by labeling all pencils to come out of the factory with an "A.W. Faber" mark. In 1840 he developed the world's first hexagonal pencil, and in 1856 he contracted for exclusive access to excellent East Siberian graphite. To top it all off, Eberhard Faber built the first mechanized pencil factory in the United States in New York in 1851. Ever since, the technology of pencils has evolved tremendously, and yet has not been able to dethrone this centuries-old design.

Herbert Allen, American, 1907–1990
Screwpull Corkscrew, 1979
Polycarbonate plastic and metal
Manufacturer: Hallen Co., USA

While mention of "cork drawers" can be found as early as in seventeenth-century texts, the first official patent was accorded in England in 1795 to the Reverend Samuel Henshall, who improved upon earlier shank-and-worm schemes by adding a simple metal button between the two. This solution first introduced the continuous clockwise motion we have become familiar with. It is impossible to count how many different corkscrew designs were introduced after that, or to list all the inventors and collectors who have dedicated their lives to these most engaging tools. But certainly, the affordable and manageable Screwpull represents one of the highest moments in corkscrew history. Herbert Allen, an inventor with a few aerospace and oil-drilling industry patents under his belt, became enraptured with wine during a trip to Europe in the 1950s. In 1975, he decided to celebrate wine in his own way, by inventing the perfect corkscrew. The plastic frame, easy to manufacture at low cost, fits easily on the neck of the bottle; the Teflon-coated helical screw penetrates the cork and is easily maneuvered via a stylish, yet ergonomically correct handle; the motion is effortless and easy; and the whole Screwpull comes apart for cleaning and storage. As dramatic as other screws might have appeared in shape, the humble Screwpull conquered the world with ease.

Italo Marchioni, Italian, 1868–1954
Ice Cream Cone, 1896
This model manufactured by Ben & Jerry's Homemade, USA

At the end of the nineteenth century, Italo Marchioni, an Italian immigrant, made and sold homemade lemon ices from a pushcart on Wall Street in New York. In 1896, he started to bake edible waffle cups with sloping sides and a flat bottom, with the intention of reducing overhead caused by lost or broken serving glasses. He patented his invention in 1903, but Marchioni's place in the history of the ice cream cone remained unnoticed for many years, with others being credited for the invention.

The great ice cream cone controversy began during the 1904 St. Louis World's Fair, which featured approximately fifty ice cream stands and a large number of waffle shops. Like everyone else, Charles Menches sold his ice cream in dishes, but one busy summer morning at the Fair, he ran out. With more than half a day of business ahead of him, he had to find an instant so-lution. Nearby was a stand where Syrian pastry maker Ernest Hamwi was selling a Middle Eastern treat called *zalabia*, consisting of a crisp, waferlike confection sprinkled with sugar. Menches rolled up the *zalabia*, scooped his ice cream on top, and ice cream cones were born, again.

On the same occasion, Abe Doumar, David Avayou, Arnold Fornachou, and brothers Albert and Nick Kabbaz claimed to have created the new treat. Doubtless, the 1904 Fair was the place where the cone became popular—it earned the moniker "the World's Fair Cornucopia."

HUMBLE MASTERPIECES   / Spark Plug

Albert Champion, French, 1878–1927
Spark Plug, ca. 1904
This model: Champion Traditional Spark Plug
Steel, copper, ceramic, and other materials
Manufacturer: Champion Spark Plug Company, USA

Spark plugs work by providing a tiny air gap between two electrodes, in which a spark for fuel ignition can be formed. Originally French, spark plugs are currently found in the engines of many vehicles, from motorcycles to airplanes. Spark plugs were used by both Charles Lindbergh and Amelia Earhart in their transatlantic flights and to fire the second and third stage rocket engines that propelled Neil Armstrong, Buzz Aldrin, and Mike Collins all the way to the moon. The model shown here is the one specified for a 1966 Porsche 911.

France dominated the spark plug market in the early 1900s. Albert Champion, a renowned French bicycle and motorcycle racer, came to America in 1899 to compete and found to his dismay that parts for the cycles he had brought over with him were difficult to find in the United States. He moved to Flint, Michigan, and in 1904 founded Champion Ignition Company for large-scale spark plug manufacturing. Problems with investors led to Champion's leaving the company, although it continued to produce spark plugs under his name.

HUMBLE MASTERPIECES / Cable Turtle

Flex Development BV, Dutch, established 1988
Cable Turtle, 1996
Thermoplastic elastomer
Manufacturer: Cleverline, the Netherlands

Thank the culturally house-proud Dutch for not liking anything too unsightly in their homes and for coming up with the Cable Turtle, an ingeniously simple case for wires that would otherwise tangle themselves up in a constantly growing mess all over the floor, table, or bookshelf. The designers realized that our lives are being dominated by electrical and electronic equipment, and rather than mourn the loss of simplicity, set out to deal with the issue gracefully.

They began experimenting with various ways of holding cables together and had the idea of turning two thermoplastic rubber shells, which could be folded inside out and then back together, enclosing bunches of wires in their turtlelike casings. The function depends on the geometry of the shells, and the company made a number of prototypes, focusing on the connection between the two shells. Because of the interior working environment mandated by the design firm, no poisonous glues or dangerous assembly methods could be used, which led the team to designing a permanent snap-fit that required no other materials or dangerous solvents. The cable turtle is available in three sizes—for large, medium, and small cable sets—and has become a hit both for its soft material and its attractive shape.

Unknown Designer
Soccer Ball, ca. 1860
This model: Nike Tiempo Classic, 2004
Polyurethane and carbon latex
Manufacturer: Nike, USA

The soccer ball has a long and colorful history of bringing people together, even inspiring occasional truces in times of war, as in a famous Christmas match that happened in 1915 near Laventie, in northern France, between a Welsh and a German battalion. The earliest ballplayers used objects ranging from pig or cow bladders to human heads. Animal bladders, eventually covered in leather, were used as balls until Charles Goodyear patented vulcanized rubber in 1836. In 1855, he designed and built the first rubber soccer ball, and in 1862 H. J. Lindon produced one of the first inflatable rubber bladders for balls. They continued to vary in size and shape until the English Football Association revised its original 1863 game rules in 1872 to include a description of the ball, agreeing that it "must be spherical with a circumference of 27 to 28 inches." The soccer ball is still the same size, but its shape and manufacture have changed multiple times since these nineteenth-century decisions. It took until the 1960s for the first completely synthetic ball to be produced, and until the 1980s for synthetic leather to replace real leather, because people thought that leather balls were more consistent in both flight and bounce.

Although balls come today in many decorative designs, the shape of the modern-day soccer ball is referred to as a "buckyball," a name inspired by American architect Richard Buckminster Fuller's experiments in maximum building with minimum material. His globe constructions consisted of series of hexagons, pentagons, and triangles that fit together to make an almost perfectly round surface, a trick the modern soccer ball, with its twenty hexagonal and twelve pentagonal surfaces, adopts. The pieces are sewn together and then inflated, and the alternation between black and white is not only for decoration but so that players can perceive swerve and spin from across the field.

Arthur A. Aykanian, American, born 1923
Spoon Straw, 1968
Polypropylene plastic
Manufacturer: Winkler/Flexible Products, USA

Straws terminating in a spoon could be found in eighteenth-century Holland, where they would be manufactured in silver, but chances are their introduction happened much earlier on, in Persia. In Victorian times, on the wave of new treatises on etiquette and table manners, specialized tableware became particularly fashionable. For spoons, this meant a whole new enlarged family of grapefruit spoons—with a serrated edge—and iced tea and soda spoons, for instance, these latter often also featuring a hollow handle that doubled as a straw. The spoon portion was worked separately and then attached to the straw until well into the twentieth century. Until, that is to say, the introduction of thermoplastics, and especially polypropylene, in 1948.

Marvin Stone, a manufacturer of cigarette holders, had introduced serially produced drinking straws in paper in 1888. In the 1930s, Joseph Friedman, of San Francisco, invented the flex-straw while hanging out in his brother's ice cream parlor. The switch to plastic made the production of the straw and the flex-straw even more massive. The industrial spoon straw was a mere step of machinery design away, just enough variation in the production to allow the end part of the plastic tube to be opened into a scoop.

Sir Henry Tate, British, 1819–1899
Sugar Cube, 1872
Manufacturer: Tate & Lyle PLC, United Kingdom

While sugar consumption in Europe has been documented since the four-teenth century, it was not until 1872 that self-made British industrialist Henry Tate, the Tate in both Tate & Lyle and the Tate Gallery, patented a method for cutting sugar into small cubes. The popularity of sugar had reached an all-time high in the eighteenth century, when Europeans developed even more of an affinity for the sweet sugarcane product than they had in the seventeenth century, when sugar was worth its weight in gold.

According to a romantic legend, sugar, now considered a New World crop, was brought over to North America by Christopher Columbus in 1493. The explorer stopped over at Gomera, one of the Canary Islands, intending to stay for only a short time when he became romantically involved with Beatrice, the island's governor. The affair lasted a month, at the end of which she gave him a gift of sugar cuttings, which he took with him to the New World and planted. In reality, Columbus was already well aware of sugar's value as a commodity, as he had been involved in shipping sugarcane from Madeira to Genoa as early as in 1478.

With the drop in price, sugar exploded in popularity in the eighteenth cen-tury, when Europeans began to include it in much of their daily intake. Jams, candy, cocoa, and processed foods became very popular, and recipes from that era often include sugar in the most unlikely meals (chicken and rice, for example). Tate realized the market for sugar cubes, and the ease of produc-tion, and hit his stride at exactly the right time with his simple yet effective manufacturing methods.

In spite of sugar's dark history in the New World, in the Old World,Tate is remembered as a great philanthropist. It is sweet to think that both the Tate Gallery in London, which opened in 1897 to display Tate's art collection, and the Liverpool University Library were built on the invention of sugar cubes.

Blomus Design, German
Stainless Steel Soap, 2001
Manufacturer: Blomus, Germany

It is hard to believe that a beautiful steel pebble can actually eliminate bad odors from one's skin. The stainless steel soap is an extension of the practice more adventurous home cooks already engaged in—rubbing their garlicky hands on the steel of their sink faucet, finding that the metal's magnetic ion properties were perfect for neutralizing odors.

HUMBLE MASTERPIECES / Flat-Bottomed Brown Paper Grocery Bag

Margaret Knight, American, 1838–1914
Charles Stillwell, American, n.d.
Flat-Bottomed Brown Paper Grocery Bag, 1883
Kraft paper
Manufacturer: Duro Bag Manufacturing Company, USA

Before Margaret Knight developed the flat-bottomed paper bag in 1870, bags were either envelopes or shapeless sacks that took on the form of whatever material they contained. Knight, a worker in a paper bag manufacture, devised a machine part that could fold and glue the bags and give them a square bottom. A natural inventor since she was a child, she went on to found the Eastern Paper Bag Company and to collect patents for twenty-six other creations.

Charles Stillwell, working in Fremont, Ohio, in 1883, also invented a machine that could make straight-sided pleated paper bags with a flat bottom, a more advanced version of Knight's bag, and called the product the "Self-Opening Sack," referring to it as "the first bag to stand upright by itself."

The bag gained popularity because merchants were able to imprint their own names and/or logo on it, which allowed them to receive free advertising simply by selling and bagging their own merchandise. Today, more than twenty-five billion paper bags are used annually. The ubiquitous bags come in fourteen stock sizes.

Richard James, American, 1914–1974
Betty James, American, born 1918
Slinky, 1945
Steel
Manufacturer: James Industries, later James Spring & Wire; now part of
Poof Toys, USA

Mechanical engineer Richard James invented the Slinky by accident, as he worked with torsion springs (springs without tension) in his workshop in Philadelphia's Cramp Shipyard. One of the springs fell off a high shelf, but instead of stopping or just floundering about as tensioned springs do, it kept moving, flipping from shelf to books to tabletop to floor. Richard showed the moving spring to his wife Betty, and both realized the accident's plaything potential (after her initial bout of skepticism). Richard spent two years figuring out the best wire gauge and proportions while Betty searched for a name, combing through the dictionary in search of a word that conjured up stealthy, sleek, and sinuous. In other words, slinky! Richard and Betty founded James Industries with five hundred dollars in 1945 and at a local machine shop made four hundred Slinkys that they demonstrated at Gimbel's Department Store in Philadelphia during the Christmas shopping season. Richard convinced a friend to attend and purchase the first Slinky, which was shown walking down a slanted board in a window. The friend complied, and all four hundred Slinkys were sold during the ninety-minute demonstration.

James Spring & Wire was founded in 1956, and continues to produce all Slinkys on the market, using original equipment designed by Richard James. He developed a machine that could churn out a Slinky in 10 seconds by turning 61 feet of wire into 80 coils. In 1960 he suffered a nervous breakdown and left his wife (and six children) to join a Bolivian cult. Betty (arguably always the brains) took over as CEO, moved the company to its current Hollidaysburg location, and replaced the original blue/black Swedish steel with silver American metal.

The amount of wire used to make Slinkys since 1943 could wrap around the earth 126 times.

Unknown Designer
Dominoes, thirteenth century
This model manufactured by Kardwell International, USA

Dominoes, in the past carved from ivory and bone and currently predominantly made of wood or plastics, were small rectangular wedges dotted with round pips of inset ebony or enamel. While the oldest domino set that resembles contemporary versions appears to be from AD 1120 China, similar objects were found in Tutankhamen's tomb, a relic from the twelfth century BC, in Egypt. While no one is quite sure where the name *domino* comes from, a predominant theory is that it came from the similarity between the black-and-white color of the blocks and what the French called priests' black-and-white hoods. The domino was also a type of mask that featured a black-and-white motif.

Dominoes developed as a way to represent and keep track of dice throws, each domino representing one of twenty-two possible results of a two-dice throw. Games developed out of the possibilities, and dominoes appeared in Europe, via Italy, in the early years of the eighteenth century. The game changed in translation from its Chinese origins to its European incarnation, particularly with the addition of a completely blank tile whose origin and purpose are still up in the air. Each number appears eight times in a domino set. Dominoes were introduced to the United States shortly after their European debut and had a slow start until the mah-jongg craze swept North America in the 1920s. Even Lyndon B. Johnson was devoted to dominoes.

HUMBLE MASTERPIECES   / Jelly Belly Jelly Beans

Herman Goelitz Rowland, American, born 1941
Jelly Belly Jelly Beans, 1976
Manufacturer: Herman Goelitz Candy Company; now Jelly Belly Candy
Company, USA

Before 1976, jelly beans had flavor only in their outer shells, with a chewy sugar syrup inside. Jelly Belly beans are flavored both in the center and in the shell, standard now but a far cry then. It takes seven days to make a Jelly Belly jelly bean. First, the center—a mix of sugar syrup and flavors—is created. The melted cooked mixture is dropped into large trays containing cornstarch in about 1,260 individual depressions sized for each jelly bean, and then cooled in a drying room. The centers are separated from the cornstarch, sent through what the company calls a "moisture steam bath" and sugar-coated, then left to rest for twenty-four to forty-eight hours. The shells are created by tumbling hundreds of pounds of centers in rotating drums with four layers of syrups and sugar, a throwback method taken from fifteenth-century French confectioners. The shells are built over a two-hour period, and are then polished by rolling the beans over each other while a confectioner's glaze is poured, a similar process to that used to polish rocks. The jelly beans are next placed in trays, where they sit for two to four days, and are then printed with the Jelly Belly name.

In 1976 the first eight flavors of Jelly Belly were very cherry, lemon, cream soda, tangerine, green apple, root beer, grape, and licorice; today there are more than forty, each one created with natural ingredients whenever possible, using for instance real peanut butter, chocolate, Anjou pear, and coconut, among other juices and extracts.

Norman Joseph Woodland, American, born 1921
Bernard "Bob" Silver, American, died 1962
Bar Code, ca. 1948

ISBN 0-609-60275-6

In 1948, the president of a local food chain asked one of the deans of the Drexel Institute of Technology in Philadelphia to develop a system for automatically reading product information during checkout. Bernard Silver, a graduate student, overheard the conversation, and joined together with his friend Norman Joseph Woodland to undertake research of his own. Woodland's first idea of using patterns of ink that would glow under ultraviolet light was discarded, proving to be too unstable and expensive. The first bar code they designed was made of a series of concentric circles. The basic representation was quite similar to the present-day bar code, a straight-line pattern with four white lines on a dark background. The inventors noted that if more lines were added, more classifications could be coded. October 20, 1949, marks the official birthday of the bar code, the day that Woodland and Silver filed a patent application for their method of classifying items based on the photo-response to a set pattern of lines or colors. But it wasn't until 1974 that the first scanner using the UPC symbol set—Universal Product Code, still in use today—was installed at Marsh's supermarket in Troy, Ohio. The first product to be scanned at the checkout counter was a ten-pack of Wrigley's Juicy Fruit chewing gum, on display at the Smithsonian Institution's National Museum of American History.

HUMBLE MASTERPIECES   / #1 Slant Tweezer

Tweezerman, Company Design, American, established 1980
#1 Slant Tweezer, ca. 1980
Stainless steel and enamel
Manufacturer: Tweezerman International, USA

Tweezers, a levered object with a set of pincers at the end that can grab onto bits and pieces from errant eyebrow hairs to tiny gemstones, are most likely derived from rudimentary tongs used as far back as 4000 BC to pick up or hold objects too hot to touch with bare hands. Cave paintings depict Stone Age people using two sticks, held together, over fire. There is documentation showing Roman shipbuilders pulling nails out of wood with pincers similar to today's tweezers, while European manuscripts from the Middle Ages also mention a tweezerlike pincer device.

The earliest tweezers used for makeup were discovered in what is now Iran, and have been attributed (by Iranians) to the Shahda people, among the first to make intricate bracelets with such tiny stones that they could only have been picked up by tools, and the first to make up their faces to such an extent that tweezers would be necessary and valued. I have chosen here to represent tweezers with the most classic design by Tweezerman, the company founded in 1980 to manufacture splinter tweezers, which is owned by the German Solingen, one of the best worldwide manufacturers of precision steel instruments.

But the tweezers family keeps growing. Scientists have recently made a pair of tweezers capable of picking up objects just five hundred nanometers (billionths of a meter) across. They call them—what else?—nanotweezers.

HUMBLE MASTERPIECES   / Java Jacket Coffee-Cup Sleeve

Jay Sorensen, American, born 1958
Java Jacket Coffee-Cup Sleeve, 1993
Recycled cardboard
Manufacturer: Java Jacket, USA

Inspiration can come in many different forms. Sometimes, the message can
be very direct. That's what happened to realtor Jay Sorensen the day in 1991
he dropped a cup of coffee on his lap because it was so hot, he could not hold
it any longer. He designed a simple sleeve of cardboard to fit around a standard coffee cup and together with his wife, Colleen, marketed it at a coffee
trade show in Seattle.

The insulating sleeve is made from waffle-textured recycled cardboard,
a very easy recipe to follow. As a matter of fact, powerful companies launched
similar products, but Sorensen's could count on a network of loyal followers
and thus managed to take care of the competition and stay in business.

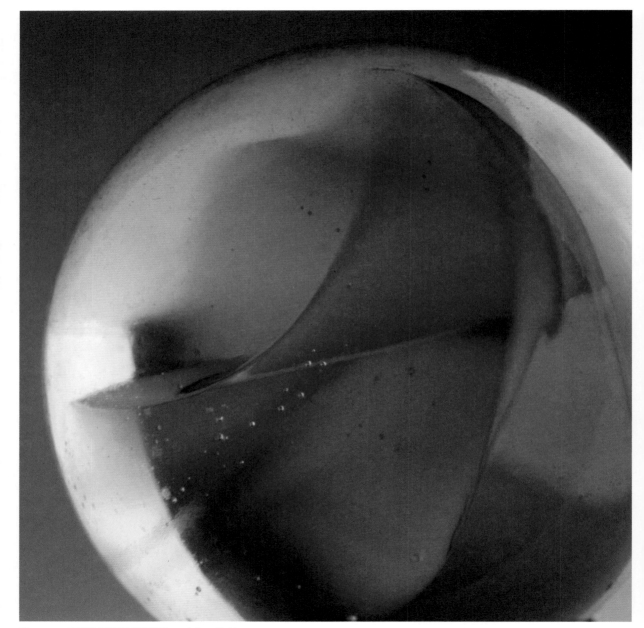

Martin F. Christensen, American, born Denmark
Glass Marbles, ca. 1906

Phenomenally popular in the first half of the twentieth century, marbles have been around as playthings and decorative objects for millennia. The ancient ones were made of either stone (inexpensive) or marble (more expensive), until porcelain and crockery versions were introduced around 1800. Clay varieties were produced in bulk from 1870 onwards, but it was the development of the glass marble that rocked the marbling world. In 1846, a German glassblower invented special shears that could be used to speed up the production of marbles, while the 1890s saw the introduction of the first machine for their mass manufacture by Martin F. Christensen. Christensen, a Danish immigrant to the United States, patented his machine in 1905, opened a factory in Ohio, and by 1914 was producing more than one million marbles a month.

The multicolored marbles we use now are made by melting glass in a furnace and mixing it with different strands of colored glass while it is flowing into a small cylinder before being dropped onto rollers that round off the cylindrical edges to form variously sized round balls.

The game of marbles was played more avidly than baseball is today by boys and girls in the 1920s and 1930s, and annual marble tournaments held by newspapers were as common as spelling bees are today. The National Marbles Tournament is still held in Wildwood, New Jersey, and the English village of Tinsley Green hosts an annual World Marble Championship. The championship is said to have begun with a sixteenth-century game in which two men vying for the same girl decided to settle it over a rousing match of marbles.

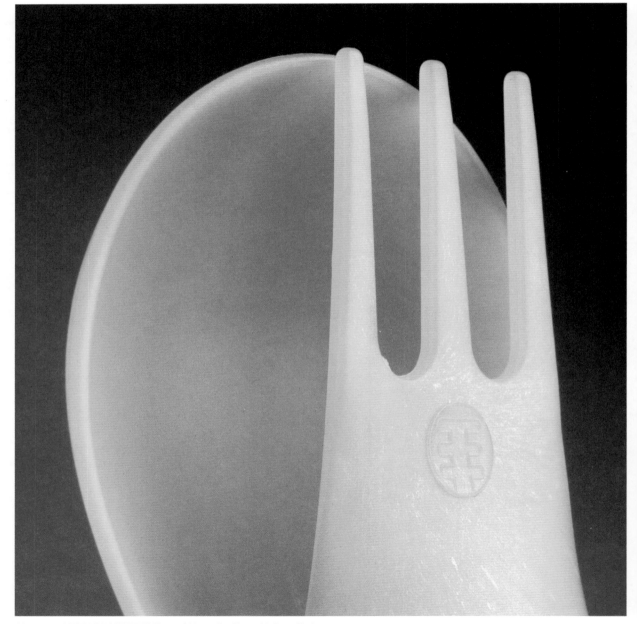

Giulio Iacchetti, Italian, born 1966
Matteo Ragni, Italian, born 1972
Moscardino Disposable Spoon/Fork, 2000
Mater-Bí (corn, grain, and potato starch) compound
Manufacturer: La Civiplast Snc di Vittorio e Ciro Boschetti, Italy

Although the noun "spork" was trademarked only in 1970, hybrid versions of spoons and forks have existed for at least 150 years. This utensil, on the other hand, has a configuration more akin to a multi-tool, with the spoon on one side and a suggestion of a fork on the other. The curious shape thus generated gives it its name, *moscardino*, which means "small squid" in Italian. The Moscardino is made of a special kind of biological plastic derived from corn, grain, and potato starch, which in certain parts of Italy are used for garbage bags in mandatory recycling programs. The cutlery is thus completely biodegradable, although it is not necessarily meant to be thrown away after its first use. Then again, because it can only withstand temperatures up to 120 degrees, it is not fit for a dishwasher. That makes it disposable in most people's book.

I♥NY IS A REGISTERED TRADEMARK AND SERVICE MARK OF THE NEW YORK STATE DEPARTMENT OF ECONOMIC DEVELOPMENT: USED WITH PERMISSION USED UNDER LICENSE BY M.B.S. LOVE UNLIMITED. INC.

Milton Glaser, American, born 1929
I ❤ NY Logo, 1976
This model: I Love NY T-shirt

Chances are you have a copy of this logo somewhere in your home, either on a T-shirt, or on a mug, or tucked inside a book or a magazine. Its ubiquity and timelessness are a sign of its incredible success as a symbol. In February 1975, the city of New York was in dire straits. With a billion-dollar deficit and bankruptcy looming, three hundred thousand workers freshly laid off, crime on the rise, and a weeklong garbage collection strike to top everything off, the city was in desperate need of an injection of hope. That is when the New York State Department of Commerce commissioned the advertising campaign that generated the most frequently imitated logo design in human history. According to Mary Wells Lawrence, one of the principals of the Wells Rich Greene agency, which got the account, many people contributed to shaping the campaign, beginning with the governor, Hugh Carey, who first pointed out that, despite everything, people still loved New York, all the way to Lawrence's colleagues, who created the initial Broadway-centered campaign with its infectious music refrain by Steve Karmen and such fixtures as Frank Sinatra, Morgan Fairchild, and Yul Brynner. Milton Glaser, a well-known graphic designer, was asked to provide the graphics for posters and other materials. He presented the agency with several detailed and full-drawn ideas, but the final momentous design happened, as many do, on a paper napkin on the spur of the moment. Eager to spread the message around the world, the City of New York did not copyright the design and let it be applied with complete license to express love for anything, anytime, a gift from New York to the world.

I ❤ NY

HUMBLE MASTERPIECES / Crown Bottle Cap

William Painter, American, 1838–1906
Crown Bottle Cap, 1892
Metal and polyvinyl chloride (PVC) plastic
Manufacturer: Crown Beverage Packaging, USA

Bottled carbonated beverages were very popular in the late nineteenth century. The only problem was their stoppers, which were unreliable and leaky. Many different closures had been developed, from simple corks to delicate porcelain caps and glass marbles within strangled-neck bottles, but only metal caps could resist the high pressure that carbonated contents exerted and seal them hermetically so they would not go flat. Metal, on the other hand, often tainted the flavor of the beverage. William Painter realized that by lining a metal lid with paper or cork, he could avoid this contamination. Painter patented the crown cap on February 2, 1892, only one of over eighty-five patents he held in his life. The crown cap was simple, single-use, economical, and designed to be completely leakproof.

Painter later developed a method for fast and easy capping and came up with a neck design for the bottle and a crimped design for the caps. A machine forced a metal disc over the thin neck of a glass bottle, crimping the edges to distribute an equal force over the entire neck. In 1898, Painter introduced a machine that both filled and closed bottles in a single process and established the crown cap as the industry standard. Since the 1960s, plastic has been used instead of the thin ring of cork that Painter had designed, and the cap now has only twenty-one points instead of Painter's original twenty-four. Other than that, the design has brilliantly withstood the test of time.

Norman & Hill, now Filofax, British, established 1921
Filofax Ring-Bound Organizer, late 1970s
Leather, steel, and paper
Manufacturer: Filofax, USA

"A file of facts" became *filofax*, and the brand name, like kleenex and band-aid, became the generic term for all paper precursors of Personal Digital Assistants. The Filofax, an exquisite symbol of the 1980s, was first designed in 1921 by the English company Norman & Hill. The design was based on the American "Organizer System" dating from World War I, and Norman & Hill's biggest client for the first twenty years of its existence was in fact the British Army, which could appreciate the regimented approach to time management, followed by churches and universities. Filofax's destiny was still tied to the vagaries of war: in 1940, the entire company was destroyed by a bombing—and in 1943, legend has it that a soldier's Filofax tucked in his short pocket deflected a bullet that would have been deadly. . . . Luckily, Norman & Hill employee Grace Scurr had retained and continuously updated all crucial information about the company in her own personal Filofax, and the company was thus able to regain steam.

The current Filofax design was introduced after Norman & Hill was bought by David and Lesley Collischon and was renamed Filofax in 1976. The design is ingenious and addictive. The outer shell can come in beautiful colors and precious leathers, but it is frequently just a functional necessity, the support for the explosion of possibilities inside. Besides the basic time management sheets and the address book, the pre-punched A5 sheets would also be provided in a delicious assortment of specialized tasks, notepads, and dividers. Travel information and maps would be offered in Filofax format, and several computer programs would be set to print out Filofax-ready data. Post-it Notes and other stickers would aid the irresistible impulse to transform this functional object into a personal artistic expression. No Palm Pilot or BlackBerry will ever be able to provide the same priority shortcuts.

Adolf Rambold, German, 1900–1996
Double-Chambered Tea Bag, 1949
Paper
Manufacturer: Teepak, Germany

The first tea bags, developed in the United States in the early 1900s, were riffs on the small silk pouches that tea merchants used to provide samples for customers. The silk was eventually replaced by muslin shortly before World War I. An automatic tea-bagging machine was produced in the early 1920s, and in 1930 the first perforated parchment paper tea bags came on the market, outshining the competition in that the material had no taste of its own, leaving the tea inside unimpaired.

In 1949, Adolf Rambold, an engineer at tea bag machine company Teekanne and former part-owner of the tea bag company Teepak, invented the double-chambered tea-bag–making machine, which led to the patent of the double-chambered tea bag at the end of the year. The bag, made from utterly taste-free filter paper, contained tea in two separate chambers, which allowed water to circulate freely around the individual tea leaves, allowing their flavor to develop more fully than when the leaves were all packed together into one bag. No adhesives were used, either, as the bag was manufactured using a series of special and complex folds, which further retained the taste-free purity of the bags.

Since 1949 most tea bags (90 percent in the United States and almost 100 percent in Europe) have been double chambered, and the mass production of the bags allowed by Rambold's machines changed tea drinking from a luxury saved for few to a drink enjoyed by everyone. Currently, 60 percent of tea produced all over the world is destined for tea bags.

Gene Hurwitt, American, 1906–1988
Boxes, ca. 1965
Acrylic plastic
Manufacturer: AMAC Plastic Products Corp., USA

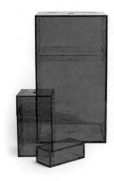

The square acrylic box, co-opted by everyone from James Bond movie set designers to a New Yorker who sells New York City garbage over the Internet, has its beginnings with Gene Hurwitt, a former fur cleaner from San Francisco who in 1960 bought a failing plastic factory named AMAC as a retirement investment, thinking of turning it around and selling it. When that proved impossible, he set out to make something special out of it.

When a pharmaceutical company asked him for square plastic boxes to efficiently store medicines, Hurwitt applied to it his interest in modern architecture, giving the final design classical proportions and a square plan. The boxes had to be transparent so that pharmacists could see through to the contents, but tinted so as to protect from damaging UV radiation. At the time, the only transparent plastic color was gold; gold they were. Hurwitt perfected his technique and began making different sizes of boxes, selling them to small arty stores in Sausalito and nearby San Francisco. After realizing the potential market, Hurwitt wanted to expand the color line. He thus approached a local ceramics company, borrowed their glazing dyes, and poured them into his plastic mix before it set. The resulting transparent colors were a novelty, and by the mid-sixties the company had twelve sizes and ten colors of boxes.

The boxes became huge icons, even more so after they were discovered by Alan Spigelman, a New Yorker who was also the first to introduce other seminal sixties designs—most notably the black light and the lava lamp—into the United States. He started selling the boxes on Canal Street, a materials haven in New York's Chinatown, while the big coup came with Andy Warhol's 1968 art piece, made for the Castelli gallery, consisting of ten artists' portraits silk-screened onto AMAC boxes.

Norman Stingley, American
Super Ball, 1965
Zectron elastomer
Manufacturer: Wham-O, USA

In the early 1960s, chemical engineer Norman Stingley accidentally created Zectron, a synthetic material compressed to the tune of 3,500 pounds of pressure per square inch that bounced uncontrollably. He offered the product to Arthur "Spud" Melin and Richard Knerr, founders of Wham-O (see page 113), and the Super Ball was born. The new toy was a sensation. A bouncing-ball craze ensued, and sales of the Wham-O Super Ball surpassed twenty million. But cheap knockoffs appeared everywhere, and before long the Wham-O Super Ball was taken off the market. Until now. After relentless pressure from fanatics, Wham-O has agreed to reissue the classic ball. The all-new Super Ball is still made from Zectron, a combination of polybutadiene and sulfur, which is compressed under 50,000 pounds of pressure. It bounces higher than any other ball, and the recovery bounce is approximately 90 percent. In one celebrated incident, a giant Super Ball, produced as a promotional item, was accidentally dropped out of a twenty-third-floor hotel window in Australia. It shot back up fifteen floors, then down again onto a parked convertible. The car was wrecked, but the ball survived the "test" in perfect condition.

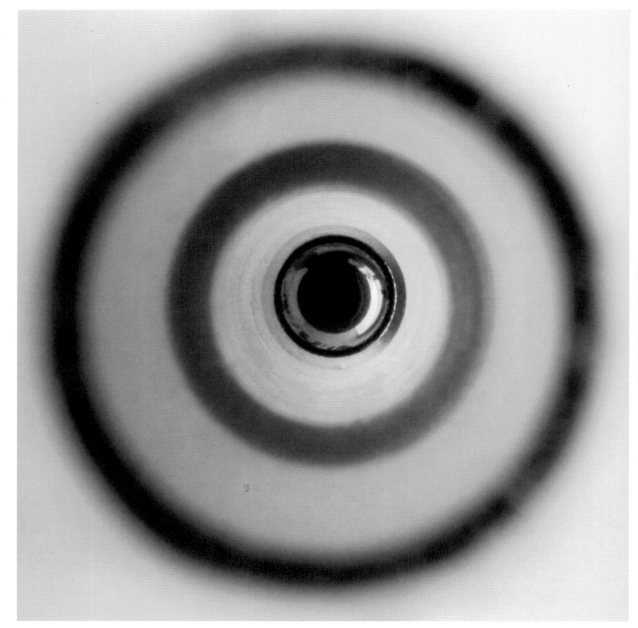

Décolletage Plastique Design Team, French
Bic Cristal, 1950
Polystyrene and polypropylene plastics, tungsten carbide
Manufacturer: Société Bic, France

In 1938, a Hungarian journalist named Laszlo Biro invented the first ballpoint pen, which used the same type of quick-drying ink employed in newspaper printing. But this thicker kind of ink could not flow from a regular nib, so Biro came up with the idea of a tiny ball that could pick up the ink from the cartridge and leave it on the paper as it rotated.

In 1945, French Baron Marcel Bich bought a factory outside of Paris to make parts for fountain pens and mechanical lead pencils. Bich obtained the patent rights to Biro's invention, and introduced his own ballpoint pen in December 1950, giving it a shortened, easy-to-remember version of his own name. The famous Bic Cristal was born and it was a dramatic improvement over any previous ballpoint pen. As a matter of fact, Bich experimented at length with materials and decided to manufacture the ball in tungsten, a much more stable metal than the brass previously used. He also employed plastic polymers of recent invention. The Bic was an extraordinary engineering feat. Currently, about fourteen million units of Bic Cristal are sold every day around the world.

Of the two holes in the Bic Cristal, the first one, in the top, was created to comply with British standards and make it easier to breathe if the pen got stuck in your throat. The second, a third of the way up the barrel, impedes a vacuum from forming within it, which would stop the ink from flowing to the nib.

Unknown Designer
Whisk, n.d.
Stainless steel

The kitchen is ripe with beautiful objects that were invented centuries ago and have long been used for the preparation of food. Some of them, for instance most wooden spoons and some copper pans, have remained the same across history. Others have evolved by taking advantage of new materials and tech-nologies, especially the introduction of stainless steel, and are hygienic, im-pervious to rust, and able to withstand high temperatures.

The whisk, a word whose Old Norse root indicates a quick movement, was first recorded as an instrument for beating eggs in 1577, although it certainly existed even before, possibly under different names according to different cul-tures. The way in which it is built, by bringing together loops of steel into a coiled handle, is elegant and simple, a luminous example of anonymous design.

HUMBLE MASTERPIECES / Solo Traveler Coffee-Cup Lid

Jack Clements, American, n.d.
Solo Traveler Coffee-Cup Lid, 1986
Polystyrene plastic
Manufacturer: Solo Cup Company, USA

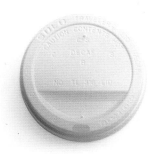

The problem is straightforward: how to prevent hot coffee—it is hard to believe that tea could have been the primal inspiration—in a portable cup from spilling and getting cold. The solutions, on the other hand, are concentrates of inventive engineering and sometimes applied decoration, and worthy of a doctoral thesis in design criticism. The coffee cup lid started as a nondescript piece of cardboard, which then became a plastic disc with concentric rings for reinforcement. The 1980s saw the introduction of small peel-off sections that left enough room for sipping without taking the lid off. But the Solo Traveler, introduced in 1986, instead of sitting flat at the rim of the cup, featured a domed configuration that its designer, Jack Clements, had devised in order to make sipping even more comfortable by accommodating not only the lips, but also the nose. As an unintended bonus, the Solo was the only one that could also accommodate the foam of the cappuccinos and lattes that were becoming the rage in those days. Its success was rapid and universal and in the cutthroat world of coffee-cup lids production, it was soon followed by several emulations. Solo, the company named after the iconic drinking paper cone it introduced in 1940, has recently introduced a new version, the Solo Traveler Plus, which allows the user to open and close the sip hole with one hand.

Iain Sinclair, British, born 1943
Flashcard, 1992
Cardboard, incandescent lightbulbs, and battery
Manufacturer: Iain Sinclair Ltd., United Kingdom

Sinclair, a prolific inventor, first thought of a flat flashlight in 1983, when Polaroid's flat batteries became available. Called Liteblade, made of stainless steel, and only 5 mm (0.2 inches) thick, his first flashlight was introduced in 1988. It was a surprise and a great success. The current Flashcard was introduced four years later. It consists of two super-bright minuscule incandescent bulbs and a dome switch, all encased in a cardboard envelope—an envelope that can be printed with patterns and corporate logos, thus opening an even wider market to its manufacturer. The Flashcard easily fits in a pocket and pressing it between thumb and forefinger turns it on. More recently, Sinclair has added to his catalog a version in translucent paper that shows the flashlight's surprising innards, as well as a version with a ruler and other measurement tools.

Art Fry, American, born 1931
Spencer Silver, American, born 1941
Post-it Note, ca. 1977
Paper and adhesive
Manufacturer: 3M, USA

Most of the objects in this book have had a significant impact on the world. They are usually the ones, like the Bic pen or the Swiss army knife, that have reached every part of the globe in their original form or in an inspired copy. They are useful, simple, and affordable revolutionary objects that have become necessary.

The Post-it Note is one of them. Many of us cannot imagine life without these "stickies." The original one is square, almost an expression of rationality, and yellow, to attract attention—and to be easy to photocopy. The manufacturer has described how its research scientist Dr. Spence Silver had first developed the technology in 1968 while conducting routine experiments on 3M acrylate adhesives. Instead of a strong adhesive, Silver concocted a removable one, composed of tiny spheres that maintained their shape and thus, although sticky individually, would not allow the paper to stick permanently.

For many years, the application of this new discovery remained unrealized until Art Fry, a new-product-development researcher at 3M, frustrated with old-fashioned paper bookmarks falling out of books, saw a way to use this experimental adhesive, which allowed the removal and reattachment of paper. First a bookmark and soon thereafter an instant memo, the Post-it Note has generated innumerable offshoots and imitations. There even exists a software program, aptly called Stickies, that allows for notes to appear as if stuck onto the computer screen. Yet, it is the original square yellow note that has become ubiquitous in contemporary life.

HUMBLE MASTERPIECES   / Bobby Pin

Unknown Designer
Bobby Pin, ca. 1920
Steel
Manufacturer: Goody Products, USA

The exact origins of the bobby pin are still vague. Bent wire hairpins originated in England in the sixteenth century, but we can be fairly certain that
their surge in popularity, and in technology, coincided with the "flapper" style
of the late teens and early twenties of the twentieth century, when hair was
often pinned closely to the head in a bobby. The straight bobby pin, crimped
and plastic-tipped in order to grip the hair as strongly as possible, was designed to stay put.

As Leonard Goodman, former head of Goody Products said, "Mechanics
serve the design and sometimes the design serves the mechanics." The company was started by his great-grandfather Henry Goodman, who sold rhine-
stone-studded hair combs on the streets of New York in 1907. The current top
producer in the United States, Goody developed the automatic manufacturing
method that starts with a 0.080 thickness wire that is flattened down to a hun-
dred-thousandth of an inch and coated before being turned into a pin. A press
then stamps the pins out of the painted length of wire, after which a short stay
in an oven hardens the epoxy resin coating and tempers the steel. The design
of a card that could have sixty or eighty pins mounted onto it—without man-
ual labor—proved the next major development. It took decades to perfect this
process, but by the time Goody was sold in 1993, the entire production of
bobby pins was mechanized to the highest possible degree.

Ross Gardner, American, 1933–2000
E-A-R Earplug, 1972
Polyurethane foam
Manufacturer: Cabot Safety Company, USA

To keep us safe from the noise pollution that comes from proximity with neighbors and traffic, as well as sometimes to tune out the white noise that has become a soundtrack to our lives, the simple earplugs have become important.

The biggest design action on the basic idea of an earplug has been devoted not to the shape, but rather to the choice of the material, which has to be not only sound absorbing, but also as hygienic as possible. While wax and clay plugs had been around for a long time, musician Ray Benner and his wife, Cecilia, were the first to manufacture them out of moldable silicone, in 1962. Ten years later, Ross Gardner was inspired by the foam used on headphones to design a new type of disposable earplugs.

The noise—and the annoyance—around us are ever increasing. Soon they'll allow mobile phones on airplanes. Mark my words: we will look at earplugs with new eyes, and find them even more beautiful and meaningful than ever.

Alfonso Bialetti, Italian, 1888–1970
Moka Express Coffeemaker, 1933
Aluminum
Manufacturer: Bialetti, Italy

This inexpensive coffeemaker, which can be found in 95 percent of the house-holds in Italy and makes the most delicious coffee, comes in four sizes: 3, 6, 9, or 12 cups—Italian espresso cups being of course the universal unit of meas-ure of Italy. In it, the water, heated in the bottom section, is forced up through the coffee grounds and then collected on top.

As a result of 1930s technology, aluminum proved to be a superior metal to steel or iron for coffee pots, because its chemical reaction with water made much better coffee. However, the Moka did not begin to achieve its universal success until the 1950s, when Alfonso Bialetti's brother Renato took over its commercialization. One last detail: the little mustached man in the logo and on every Moka is the inventor himself.

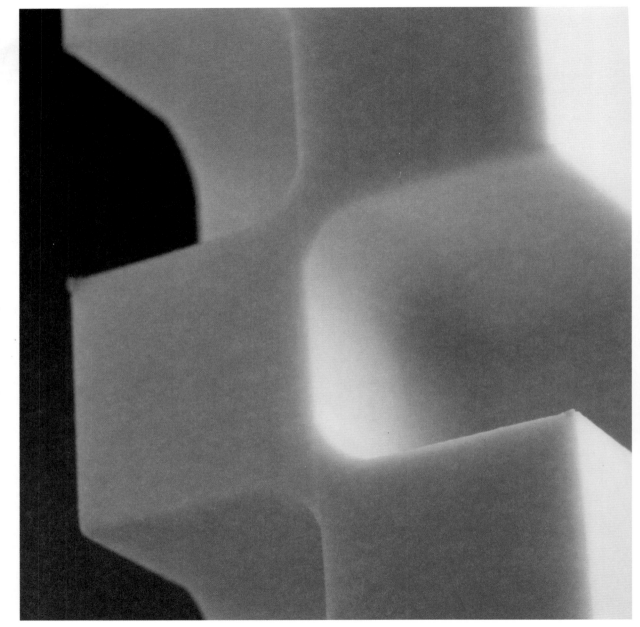

Hideo Kanbara, Japanese, born 1978
Kadokeshi Plastic Eraser, 2001
Rubber
Manufacturer: Kokuyo Co., Japan

Most rectangular erasers have eight corners. After days of rubbing out pencil mistakes, the corners become flattened and the erasers are not as precise as we would want them to be. The Kadokeshi eraser has twenty-eight corners, a feat of eraser engineering that in no small way improves the work of earnest designers and writers—those who spend hours a day drawing, erasing, writing, rethinking. The name comes from two Japanese words: *kado*, meaning "corner," and *keshigomu*, meaning "eraser." The eraser is made of ten staggered cubes, joined together to create an angular mishmash of empty space and rubber, its twenty-eight small corners much easier to work with than a typical eraser's large eight.

The design was widely praised shortly after the eraser had been developed, but the prototypes made of the same material as other erasers tore apart during use, due to the reduced supporting area around any given corner. The manufacturer, Kokuyo, adjusted the chemical makeup of the eraser, resulting in a much harder material that stood up to the constant use its design entailed. The success of the Kadokeshi eraser inspired the manufacturer to begin offering a Kokuyo Design Award in 2002, inviting the public to submit ideas for a product that would change the drawing and writing world as much as the eraser had.

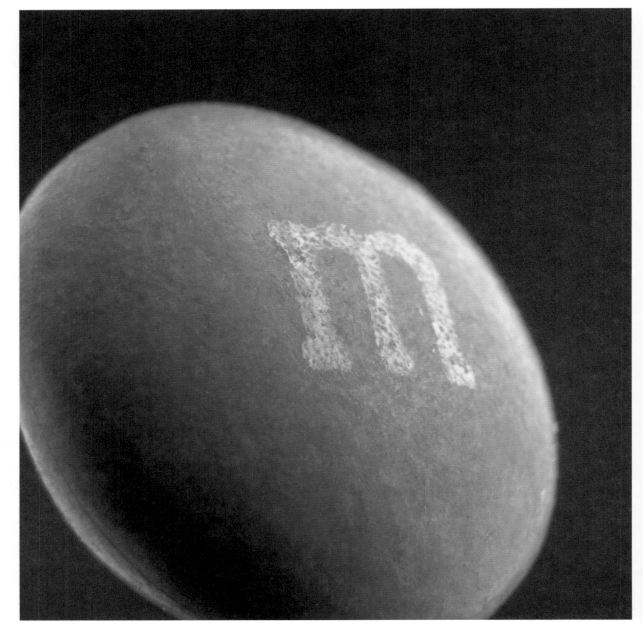

Forrest Mars, American, 1904–1999
M&M's, late 1930s
Manufacturer: Mars, USA

Legend has it that the idea for M&M's Plain Chocolate Candies was born against the backdrop of the Spanish Civil War (1936–1939). Apparently, while on a trip to Spain, Forrest Mars Sr.—the first M of M&M, the second his associate Bruce Murrie—saw soldiers eating pellets of chocolate covered with a hard sugary coating, which prevented the candy from melting. Inspired by this idea, he went back to his kitchen and invented the recipe for M&M's. M&M's were first sold to the public in 1941, packaged in cardboard tubes. Sent to the military as a convenient snack that traveled well in any climate, they soon became a favorite of American soldiers serving in World War II. By the late 1940s they became widely available to the public. In 1948, the packaging changed from a tube to the brown plastic pouch we know today. In 1954, M&M's Peanut Chocolate Candies were introduced. That same year, the M&M's brand characters and the famous slogan "The milk chocolate that melts in your mouth, not in your hand" were both trademarked.

More recently, M&M has kept us on the edge of our seats by adding new colors (grey and pink for instance) in limited editions, and discontinuing others.

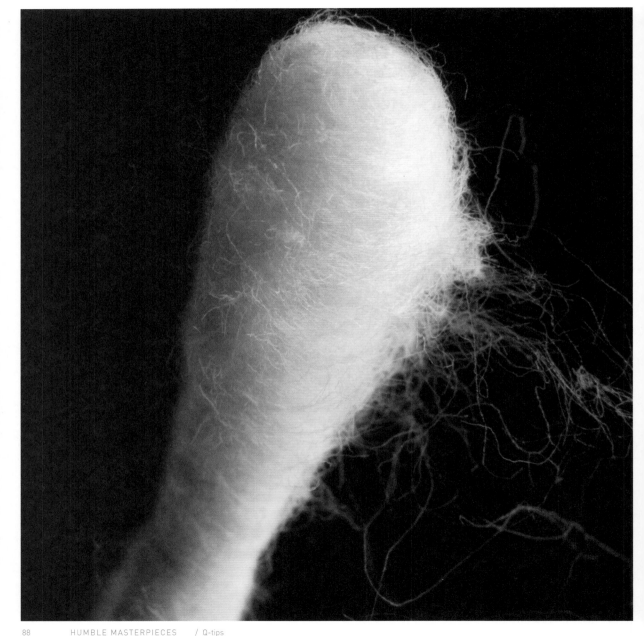

Leo Gerstenzang, American, born Poland, n.d.
Q-tips, 1923
Cotton and paper
Manufacturer: Leo Gerstenzang Infant Novelty Company; now Q-tips, USA

Leo Gerstenzang conceived the ready-to-use cotton stick upon observing his wife applying wads of cotton to toothpicks to clean their baby's ears. In 1923 he founded the Leo Gerstenzang Infant Novelty Co. While Q-tips appear to be a simple concept, Gerstenzang spent several years perfecting the design. Safety was the main concern. He replaced the original wooden stick with a white cardboardlike material, fearing that wood might possibly splinter. Having an equal amount of cotton on both ends and making sure that it could not fall off and get stuck in the ear were also subjects of much study. The product was originally called Baby Gays, but in 1926 the name was changed to Q-tips Baby Gays, and then later on to just Q-tips. The "Q" in the name Q-tips stands for quality, and the word "tips" describes the cotton swabs on the ends of the stick.

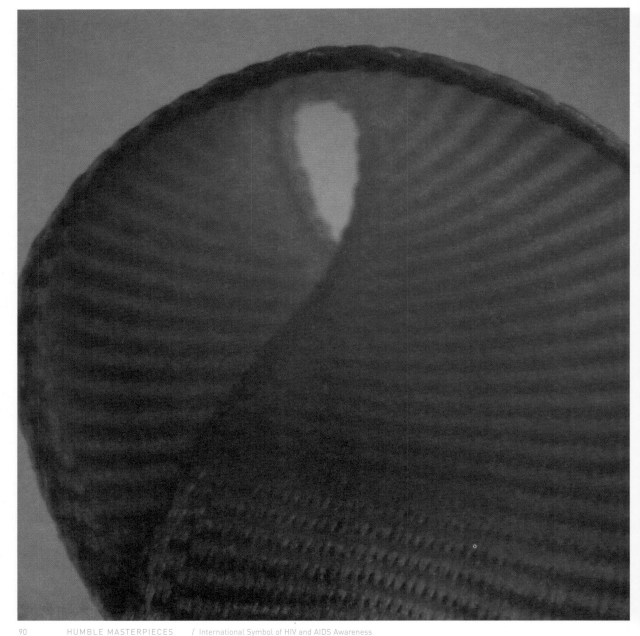

HUMBLE MASTERPIECES / International Symbol of HIV and AIDS Awareness

Visual AIDS Artists Caucus, American, established 1988
International Symbol of HIV and AIDS Awareness, 1991
Red ribbon and safety pin

The red AIDS ribbon addresses a profoundly difficult cause with a disarmingly simple design. An inverted V made of six inches of material, folded over and fastened at the intersection with a tiny safety pin, the red ribbon represents solidarity with the AIDS awareness movement and compassion for victims of the disease. The color red conjures associations with disparate but ultimately united aspects of the disease and its attributes: blood, passion, anger, and—above all—love. While its significance was later divorced from any political agenda, the ribbon was inspired by the yellow ribbon worn by concerned citizens as a sign of solidarity with the soldiers sent to the Gulf War in 1990.

The design is the product of collaboration among the members of the Visual AIDS Artists Caucus, a boundary-breaking group of artists who in April 1991 produced this conceptual artwork—an unpatented symbol that could be manufactured anywhere, by anyone. Two weeks later, Jeremy Irons publicly introduced the ribbon at New York City's Tony Awards, and later on, also on the big screen, bringing the idea full circle from its artistic origins to its artsy public.

The ribbon was quickly adopted all over the world, iconic and visually enticing enough to bypass cultural resistance even in the most reluctant countries. It has become a universal symbol. Homeless and unemployed women began to produce the symbolic ribbons, and the United States Postal Service printed a stamp with the image of the ribbon. Other awareness groups have taken inspiration from the simplicity and effectiveness of this idea and have incorporated the ribbon, giving it different symbolic colors (pink for breast cancer, yellow in memory of prisoners of war, and more recently, purple in remembrance of the victims of 9/11). While the ribbons can be worn daily, they are out in fullest force on December 1, World AIDS Day.

Sherman L. Kelly, American, 1869–1952
Ice Cream Scoop, 1935
Aluminum
Manufacturer: The Zeroll Co., USA

While on vacation in Florida, Sherman L. Kelly of Toledo, Ohio, decided to buy some ice cream and watched the attendant struggling to scoop it out of the container. It was the combination of having to wait for his ice cream cone and sympathy for the poor chap that inspired him to design what he ambitiously decided would be the world's best ice cream scoop. The two biggest problems with existing scoops were that they either relied on a swivel click and lock mechanism which could catch, rust, or break, or they didn't, and the ice cream therefore often ended up sticking to the scoop.

Kelly's scoop, manufactured by Zeroll, the company he founded in 1935 to market his invention, had no moving parts and was made out of lightweight and strong aluminum alloy, impervious to rust. The kicker of genius was an antifreeze liquid contained within the handle of the scoop, which would be warmed upon contact with the user's hand and transmit just enough warmth to the bowl of the scoop so that ice cream curled into it could effortlessly fall off into the waiting cone or dish. Good for the servers, but even better for the owners, the scoop not only reduced the amount of work, but also produced up to 20 percent more servings per gallon. The ice cream that with other scoops was compressed and packed together, necessitating more in order to make a decent-looking portion, gently curls into the Zeroll scoop like a giant wave. The Zeroll scoop works for both left- and right-handed people, in a rare example of design equality.

Pierre (Dom) Pérignon, French, 1638–1715
Champagne Cork, seventeenth century
Cork

Champagne corks, like champagne itself attributed to a blind Benedictine monk from the seventeenth century, Dom Pérignon, start out as straight corks, similar to those used in still wine but twice as large. They are crushed into the bottle neck, after which the remaining cork is jammed down, forming a mushroom-shaped head. The corks are not solid, but are rather disks of cork separated by a cork mash, which allows for much greater compression. Once the corks are smashed into the bottle necks, they are fitted with a wire muzzle that is tightened around the cork and the bottle neck, preventing the cork from flying out under pressure.

Cork comes from cork trees, a species of oak that grows primarily in Spain, Portugal, and Italy and that sometimes lives to be 170 years old. Bottle corks are manufactured by stripping the bark, drying it for six months, boiling it for ninety minutes, drying it for another three weeks, and cutting the strips into cork shapes, approximately 40 percent of which end up being usable. Cork is used because it prevents oxygen from entering the bottle and spoiling the wine, and the corks' easy compressibility means that they can be squeezed into bottle necks after which they expand, ensuring a tight fit.

Sometimes however, corks do fly; the longest recorded distance for a cork exploding out of the bottle was 177 feet and 9 inches.

Earl S. Tupper, American, 1907–1983
Tupperware Storage Bowls, 1946
Polyethylene plastic
This model: Mini Wonderlier Bowls
Manufacturer: Tupperware, USA

Earl Silas Tupper, a chemist who spent one year at chemical powerhouse DuPont before opening his own company in 1938, invented what became known as Tupperware, but it was the neighborhood party marketing of his onetime collaborator Brownie Wise that put the product on the consumers' map.

Tupper was experimenting with injection-molded polyethylene in the early 1940s and created a range of household objects, the first being a rainbow-colored drinking glass. In 1942 he founded Tupper Corporation and in 1946 he released his first designs, which included a coffee cup and glasses with scalloped edges that made for easier sipping. Tupper's landmark invention was the Tupper Seal, an airtight polyethylene enclosure similar to the vacuum seal on a paint can, for which he was awarded a patent in 1947. He began manufacturing the semi-opaque pastel-colored food containers—a contemporary version of which is shown here—and while they later became the cultural epitome of suburban mid-century American life, they were slow to catch on. It took a middle-aged divorced mother named Brownie Wise to push Tupperware to the place it occupies today, both in practice and in the popular culture. She sold Tupper's ware independently through a company called Stanley Home Products and realized that throwing parties for neighboring housewives was the best way to sell Tupper's invention, as well as other products from the Stanley catalog. Her idea made such a positive dent in the company's profits that Tupper hired her to apply her sales savvy exclusively to his line. In 1958, seven years after her hire, the Tupper corporation was sold to Rexall Company for sixteen million dollars. It was the Rexall Company that named the household item Tupperware and developed a clearer and less waxlike version of the containers. The containers, now articulated in several specialized lines, are still ubiquitous in households, suburban and urban, across America and around the world today.

Kenji Ekuan, Japanese, born 1929
GK Design Group, Japanese, established 1953
Kikkoman Soy Sauce Dispenser, 1961
Glass and polystyrene plastic
Manufacturer: Kikkoman Corporation, Japan

Post–World War II Japan found itself in an identity crisis, its citizens having to hold on tight to the elements of their history, culture, and cuisine despite the desolate feelings and the practical effects brought by a devastating and momentous defeat. Soy sauce, used for hundreds of years as a staple of the Japanese diet, found itself at the forefront of this historical necessity, but the brand needed a boost of modernity.

Soy sauce was originally sold in 1.8 liter bottles, both unwieldy and unsightly, and the design of a new bottle rested on fixing those two problems. Kenji Ekuan, a Buddhist monk working at GK Design Group in Japan, set out to redesign the soy sauce dispenser for the company Kikkoman.

The bottle had to fit in with the minimalist Japanese aesthetic while at the same time being a comfortable fit for the user, a double deal closed by the design of a wide-bottomed bottle that tapers at the neck and ever so slightly funnels out at the very top. The see-through glass, functional in that it allows the consumer to see how much soy sauce is left and beautiful in its stirring simplicity, contrasts with a bright red cap that adds visual depth to the dark oily sauce. Designing the spout proved the greatest challenge, as soy sauce has about as much viscosity as wine: none at all. Ekuan developed close to one hundred models, none of which succeeded in both preventing drip and controlling flow. An inward angle on the tip of the spout proved the right solution, preventing the sauce from pooling in the spout and dripping onto the table. Shipping volume has reached 250 million bottles, roughly twice Japan's population.

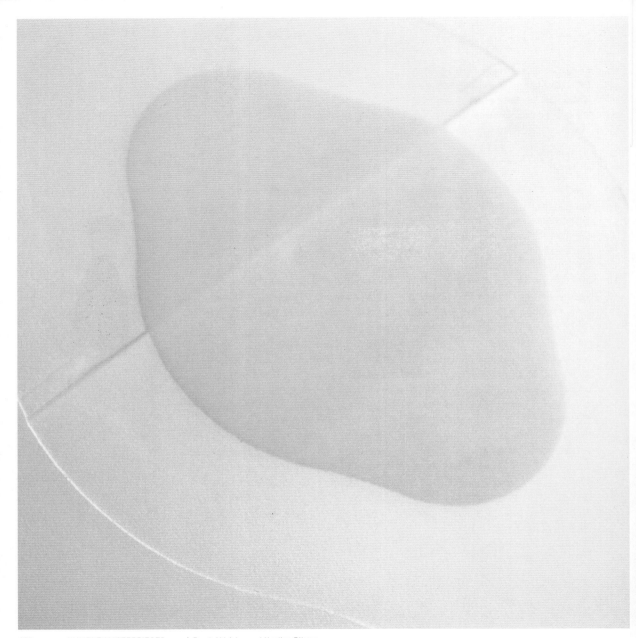

Coloplast, Danish, established 1957
Band-Aid Advanced Healing Blister, 2002
Compeed hydrocolloid gel
Manufacturer: Johnson & Johnson, USA

Few new products have encountered as much universal enthusiasm as these blister healing adhesive strips, hailed as a miraculous invention by surfers, skiers, trekkers, and respectable sandal-wearing ladies alike. Coloplast, a Danish company specializing in health-care products, first developed Compeed (a special form of hydrocolloid, a substance that forms gel with water) for ulcer dressing in hospitals, and then applied it to a more mundane version sold in drugstores for the treatment of common wounds, especially blisters. Since Johnson & Johnson purchased the invention, we can now officially call it a Band-Aid.

The Band-Aid is flexible and tapered at the edges, so it conforms to the skin almost perfectly, like an artificial, yet hygienic soft scab. Its surface is waterproof and washable, so it can be left on for days at a time. Looking like a translucent sticky slug, once it is applied to the blistered region, it draws the fluids from the injured skin and turns them into a padding gel. After a few days, when the Band-Aid is removed from the healed skin, a ghost of the absorbed blister remains impressed in the gel.

Makoto Hagiwara, American, born Japan, 1854–1925
Fortune Cookie, 1914
Flour, eggs, sugar, butter, salt

The fortune cookie is most definitely not Chinese in origin. It is widely believed to be the invention of Makoto Hagiwara, the Japanese landscape designer who created San Francisco's Golden Gate Park's Tea Garden at the end of the nineteenth century, and to be inspired by a traditional offering made at Shinto shrines during the New Year's festivities. The fortune cookie has made a remarkable reverse immigration through its almost one hundred years of existence. The Chinese affiliation was supported by an ancient legend claiming that Chinese soldiers in the thirteenth century slipped rice paper messages into mooncakes in order to secretly coordinate their defenses against marauding Mongolian invaders (who thankfully did not like mooncakes), a tradition imported by the Chinese immigrants who built the great railroads from the Sierra Nevada to California in the nineteenth century.

The cookie that Hagiwara served to rousing success debuted at the 1915 Panama-Pacific Exhibition. In the 1920s, David Jung, a Los Angeles–based baker and restaurateur, began making his own version, producing around three thousand cookies an hour through his Hong Kong Noodle Company. Fortune cookie factories soon opened all over the state, and gradually throughout the country. A machine that automatically inserted the fortune and folded the cookie was invented in the 1960s by Edward Louie of San Francisco. It took until 1993 for the first fortune cookie company to open in China.

The fortunes contained within the cookies have carried the signs of their times. Jung at first based the fortunes on passages from the Bible and quotes from Aesop, but in the more playful 1950s, he opened his enterprise to fortune-writing contests. In the 1960s and '70s, the radical culture was reflected in the zaniness of the fortunes. The moneygrubbing '80s brought with them fortunes inscribed with supposedly lucky lottery numbers. Today, the fortunes have returned to a blend of straight-up advice and incomprehensible whimsy.

Many Designers
Condom, ca. 1930
This model: Durex Flavored Condom
Latex
Manufacturer: Durex, USA

The condom is one of the designs without which our world would be a very different (and much more populated) place. The earliest recorded condoms were animal bladders used by the Egyptians in the thirteenth century BC, while Eastern legend has it that the Chinese used oiled silk paper and the Japanese either thin leather or thin tortoiseshell.

Current iterations of the condom begin in the mid-sixteenth century with Italian anatomist Gabriele Falloppio, who described his invention of a medicated linen sheath to protect against syphilis. The name "condom" is apocryphally attributed to the Earl of Condom, who in the seventeenth century was asked by King Charles II to develop something that would protect him from the syphilis his many mistresses might be carrying. The Earl's sheath, made of sheep's intestine, caught on. Even Casanova, the most famous of promiscuous men, used the prophylactic, referring to it as his "English Riding Coat."

Condoms were still far from foolproof, but the introduction of vulcanized rubber in the 1840s made their manufacture easier and their performance more reliable. Reuse, however, was still considered standard, and men were encouraged to use the condoms over and over again until they broke. The first newspaper ad for a condom appeared in 1861. Frederick Killian of Ohio was the first to test a hand-dipped latex condom in 1919, and by the 1930s, the technology of latex—an emulsion of rubber in water that made for a much thinner and more pliable product—had developed up to the point that condoms were similar to what we use today. In the 1950s the reservoir tip and sensation-deadening condom were introduced, while in 1957 Durex introduced the first lubricated model in England. The condom is blessed by current technological strides, offering textures, colors, and sometimes even flavors.

Otto Frederick Gideon Sundback, Canadian, born Swedish, 1880–1954
Zipper—Separable Fastener, 1913
This model: fabric and aluminum
Manufacturer: YKK Corporation, Japan

For the world-changing zipper, we have to thank Elias Howe, the inventor of the sewing machine, Whitcomb Judson, marketer of the "Clasp Locker," and, finally and most crucially, Gideon Sundback, who took off on the earlier prototypes to create the "Separable Fastener," patented in 1917.

Judson developed the Clasp Locker, a complicated hook-and-eye shoe fastener, in the 1890s, debuting it—to little success—at the Chicago World's Fair in 1892. He started the Universal Fastener Company and hired Gideon Sundback, a Swedish-born Canadian immigrant, to work for it. Speeding things along, Sundback married the plant manager's daughter, which, along with good design skills, led him to being named head designer of the company. Sundback's wife died in 1911, which drove the grief-stricken inventor to the design table in full force. By December of 1913 he had designed what we know today as the modern zipper.

He increased Judson's number of fastening elements from four per inch to ten or eleven, and developed two facing rows of teeth that were pulled into a single zipped-up piece by the hanging-tab slider. Once the patent was in place in 1917, Sundback developed a manufacturing machine that took a Y of wire, cut scoops from it, pushed together the scoop dimple and nib, and clamped each scoop onto cloth tape to produce a continuous zipper chain. Within the first year of operation, this zipper-making machinery was producing hundreds of feet of fastener per day. Part of the success of the zipper is attributable to its name, which came from the B. F. Goodrich Company, which co-opted Sundback's fastener for use on the company's new type of rubber boots. For the first years of the zipper, boots and tobacco pouches were the two chief uses, and it took twenty years to convince the fashion industry to jump on board the by then not-so-new fastener.

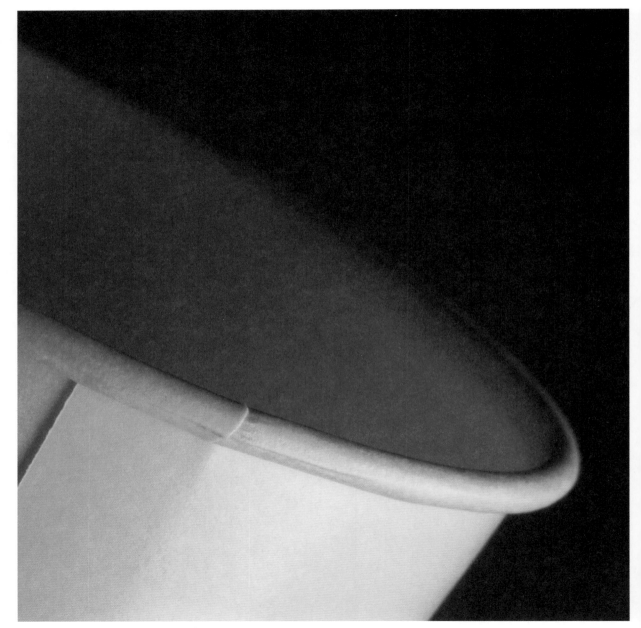

Lawrence Luellen, American, n.d.
Dixie Paper Cups, 1908
Manufacturer: Dixie Paper Cup Company; now Georgia-Pacific Corporation, USA

In the years leading up to the twentieth century, people frequently drank from communal water barrels with shared metal cups. In 1907, Lawrence Luellen, a Bostonian, became interested in developing a clean and hygienic individual paper drinking cup. After many attempts at finding investors and launching a company, Luellen established the American Water Supply Company with brother-in-law Hugh Everett Moore as director. Luellen developed a water-cooling dispenser that came with disposable cups, while Moore developed a public health education campaign about the benefits of using your own individual cup.

In 1910, they incorporated the Individual Drinking Cup Company and in 1912 they launched the Health Kup, a fixture of their first semiautomatic machine, which later became standard when the devices were put into trains. World War I brought the flu epidemic, and with it a higher demand for individual paper cups. Hugh Moore, always the business side of the operation, changed the name to set it apart from any competition, and in 1919 the Health Kup became the Dixie Cup, as it is still known today. Business expanded again when Moore and Luellen discovered that the cups could be used not only for water, but also for ice cream, and the mid-century soda fountain culture caught on quickly. In 1957 the American Can Company purchased what was by then called the Dixie Cup Company.

Unknown Designer
Bead Frame Abacus, ca. 3,000 BC
Wood, metal, and beads

The Chinese are credited for many great inventions and many of these, for instance noodles and the abacus, have remained unchanged and are still in use today, a testament to the timelessness of good design. While counting and calculating were operations initially performed by matching two sets of objects—say a certain number of stones to indicate a certain number of sheep—the abacus introduced the idea of positional notation by allowing one stone in a particular position on the table to represent a grouping of objects in the counted set. That is why it has been called by some "the first personal calculator."

Just like a good personal calculator, it is indeed portable and sturdy, made as it is of a wood frame and of thirteen metal wires, with seven beads running on each wire. A horizontal line divides the abacus between heaven and earth, with only two beads admitted into heaven.

The abacus is not a computing machine, but rather a means for people to keep track of numbers while they compute. For this reason, not only does it take some getting used to, but also it relies on a person's computational abilities. But in the hands of a skilled user, it becomes as magical and quick as a silent musical instrument.

Walter Frederick Morrison, American, born 1920
Warren Franscioni, American, 1917–1974
Frisbee, 1948
Polyethylene plastic
Manufacturer: Wham-O, USA

In the 1870s, a baker named William Russell Frisbie, owner of the Frisbie Baking Company of Bridgeport, Connecticut, started printing the family name in relief on the bottoms of the light tin pans in which his company's home-made pies were sold. Over time, Mr. Frisbie's pies were sold throughout Connecticut, including on many college campuses. Yale students claim to be the first to discover that the empty pie tins sailed through the air and could be tossed and caught.

In 1948, a building inspector and flying-saucer enthusiast from California named Walter Frederick Morrison and his partner, Warren Franscioni, designed a saucerlike plastic disc for playing catch, and aptly called it Flying Saucer, a name inspired by the country's obsession with UFOs after the 1947 sightings in Roswell, New Mexico. In 1955, Morrison sold the idea, now called Pluto Platter, to Wham-O cofounders Arthur "Spud" Melin and Rich Knerr, who are famous for having introduced to the market not only the Frisbee, but also the Hula-Hoop, the Super Ball, and the Water Wiggle. Two years later, the first Wham-O Pluto Platter was introduced to the market.

Knerr came up with a perfect new name for his product while on a pro-motional tour around Ivy League campuses. Students told him about the pie-plate-tossing craze, and how they had been calling it "frisbie-ing" for years. Knerr purposely misspelled it and quickly trademarked it as "Frisbee."

Thomas Alva Edison, American, 1847–1931
Incandescent Lightbulb, 1879
Glass, tungsten, and aluminum
Manufacturer: Edison General Electric; now GE Lighting, USA

While many people were involved in the development of the incandescent lightbulb, only one person, Thomas Alva Edison, is credited with the final step that completed the design. The icon that symbolizes, the aha! of creative discovery was not concocted in a blink. To the contrary, it took the patient work and experimentation of a long army of scientists and inventors. We can name just a few here.

The lightbulb's development extended from British chemist Humphry Davy, who in 1809 invented the first electric light by connecting two wires to a battery and placing a charcoal strip between the two wires; to Warren de la Rue, who in 1820 enclosed a costly platinum coil in a tube and passed electric current through it; all the way Henrich Globel, a German watchmaker who in 1854 invented what came to be considered the first "true" lightbulb, a glass bulb with carbonized bamboo filament as the glowing charge conductor. This marked the end of the design phase and the beginning of the filament search.

In 1878, Englishman Joseph Wilson Swan invented more practical and longer-lasting filaments with each turn and demonstrated his perfected bulb in Newcastle in January 1879. Swan was first, but it was Edison who flew with it. The American hero, working in 1879 from the patented design he had purchased in 1875, developed a carbon filament that burned for forty hours, and placed it in an oxygenless vacuum bulb invented in 1875 by Herman Sprengel. He demonstrated his design in October 1879. By 1880, Edison had improved his lightbulb until it could burn for over 1,200 hours, by using a bamboo-derived filament. In 1910 William David Coolidge finally hit upon using a tungsten filament, which outlasted all other prototypes developed until then, and at last made the production costs practical. Although the technology has evolved dramatically since then, the shape of the original lightbulb lives on.

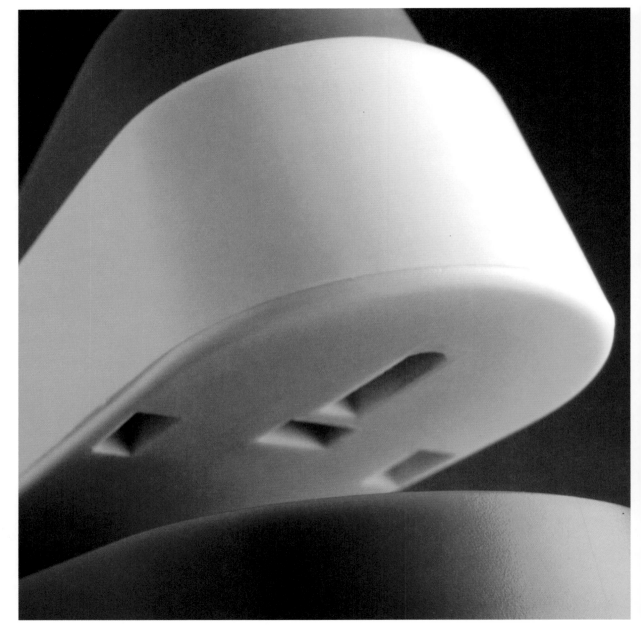

Walter Windisch, n.d.
Stapleless Stapler, ca. 1993
Plastic
Manufacturer: Kikkerland, USA

The first time is always awesome. One presses a stapler expecting upon re-
lease to find a metal fastener holding the paper sheets together, and instead
the device reveals magically punched and folded tabs out the paper itself,
which lock the sheets to each other.

The very first stapleless stapler was introduced in 1909 as the Clipless
Fastener, followed a short year later by the Bump Company's Paper Fastener.
Both methods of paper fastening were not so different from how the stapleless
stapler currently works, and rely on the natural tensile properties of paper.

Walter Hunt, American, 1795–1859
Safety Pin, 1849
Steel
This model manufacutured by A. Meyers & Sons Corp., USA

Murphy's Law concludes that the more important the occasion, the more likely the dress to rip. No bridesmaid/prom queen/fashionista is safe to get dressed without the old-fashioned standby of the safety pin, which has its earliest beginnings as a way for a prolific but poor inventor to get out of debt.

Walter Hunt, a New York mechanic, built America's first sewing machine but decided, in a fit of unlikely-for-inventors caring for the economy of others, that he didn't want to patent his invention, thinking it would lead to the immediate unemployment of hand-sewing seamstresses. His refusal to patent the sewing machine and his other inventions led to a life of debt. He found himself one day twisting a piece of wire for three hours, fiddling around as he contemplated how to pay off an outstanding debt of fifteen dollars.

After twisting the wire this way and that in abstract thought, he found that if he coiled part of the wire into a spring at one end and into a clasp and point at the other, the point of the wire would be forced into the clasp by the spring, and more importantly, forced to remain. The spring, equidistant from both point and clasp, put equal tension onto both sides, which forced the two ends together, eliminating any danger from the sharp wire point. Hunt patented his design on April 1, 1849, and sold the patent for four hundred dollars, more than paying off the debt that had led to his inspiration.

Enric Bernat i Fontlladosa, Spanish, 1923–2003
Chupa Chups Lollipop, 1958
Manufacturer: Granja Asturias; now Chupa Chups, Spain

Enric Bernat, a third-generation candy maker, took over an ailing Spanish confectionery and eliminated most of its two hundred products to focus on a single line of lollipops. "I was surprised that there was no candy made for children, when they are the main consumers. The existing ones did not fit well in their mouths, it got their hands dirty, and caused problems for their mothers. This is why I had the idea of putting it on a stick," Bernat said. "It would be like having candy with a fork." The first Chupa Chups, whose name comes from the Spanish verb *chupar*, which means "to lick," went on sale in 1958. The company instructed retailers to place the lollipops as close to the cash register as possible—a break from the traditional policy of keeping candy in glass jars behind counters, out of children's reach. Bernat knew that his company and innovative product needed a strong logo by which it could be easily identified. In 1969 he went to his friend the artist Salvador Dalí, who immediately drafted an idea on newspaper. Within an hour, the famous daisy-patterned wrapper was born, still one of the most recognized logos in the world.

Augustin-Jean Fresnel, French, 1788–1827
Fresnel Lens, 1822
This pocket-size model: acrylic plastic
Manufacturer: 3M, USA

French physicist Augustin-Jean Fresnel, who studied light and optics, developed a new type of compound lens for use in lighthouses when he was elected Lighthouses Commissioner in 1819. Whereas the previous lighthouse light source was diffracted and diffused, the Fresnel lens, first used in 1822, focused all of the light sent through the lens toward the center. This invention allowed the bright beam created from the concentration of the light to be seen from as far as twenty miles away, more than enough for any passing ship to be warned.

The Fresnel lens is flat on one side and ridged on the other, sliced into numerous concentric rings, each slightly thinner and at a different angle than the next. The same principle of magnification of light was applied to the magnification of an image, and the Fresnel lens was co-opted by stamp collectors and entomologists, as well as in the manufacture of spotlights, overhead projectors, and car headlights. Because it needs etching only on one side, the lens can easily be accommodated in convenient small sizes.

Duracell, American, established 1944
Duracell AA Battery, 1960
Steel and other materials
Manufacturer: Duracell, USA

From the moment in 1748 when the prolific inventor Benjamin Franklin coined the term to describe an array of charged glass plates, the battery underwent centuries of development and refinement. Let us here jump from Italian Alessandro Volta's first full-fledged battery in 1800 all the way to the early 1920s, when Samuel Ruben, a scientist, and Philip Rogers Mallory, a manufacturer of tungsten filament, met and began collaborating. Their partnership of genius and finance lasted until 1975, when Mallory died.

Ruben was a very prolific inventor. As an example, during World War II he devised a mercury cell that contained more power capacity in less space. It was more durable, an especially relevant consideration in times of war when the soldiers needing power had to spend time in the harsh climates of North Africa and the South Pacific. The traditional zinc carbon batteries, the most common type of batteries also today, wouldn't have been able to hold up under such stringent conditions.

In the 1950s, Ruben introduced the alkaline manganese battery, but in the end it was Eastman Kodak's introduction of the built-in flash camera that led to the small Duracell AA. The camera's flash required more power than the typical zinc carbon battery could provide, which led Ruben to develop strong alkaline manganese batteries that were small enough to fit into the cameras. Mallory produced the batteries that Ruben designed, and the Duracell brand was formally created in 1964.

Unknown Designer
Cubic Numbered Dice, between 300 BC and AD 300
This model: Precision Casino Dice
Cellulose acetate
Manufacturer: Kardwell International, USA

The ancient game of betting on chance combinations of numbers originates from the attempt to interrogate the gods to foretell good or bad luck for human enterprises by throwing objects (sticks, shells, or bones, for instance) and reading the results. From its religious beginnings to its gambling incarnation, the game of dice has accompanied the history of mankind. Ancient Egyptians as early as 2000 BC, and then ancient Greeks and Romans used all sorts of objects with a roughly rectangular shape, such as cow or mutton knucklebones, sheep anklebones, and their imitations made of terra-cotta. In some cases, numbers were assigned to the long faces of these tablets. American Indians, Aztec and Mayans, and several African tribes instead played using fruit kernels, bones, shells, or animal teeth. The modern cubic die numbered on all six faces comes from Asia, in particular Korea and India, where it is mentioned in the *Mahabharata*, the Sanskrit epic that was composed between 300 BC and AD 300.

The modern die is numbered on all of its faces, from one to six, with all combinations of opposing faces adding up to seven. Ordinary dice, not fit for use in casinos or by professional gamblers, often have rounded edges and recessed dots. Made of diverse materials, from plastics to wood and glass, they are considered lower-grade because their weight is not perfectly distributed—as a matter of fact, the die is lighter on the side of the face with six carved-out dots, opposite by definition to the face carrying only one. Precision casino dice are instead perfectly calibrated, their edge razor-sharp, and the applied pips close to the edge. They usually measure ¾ inch.

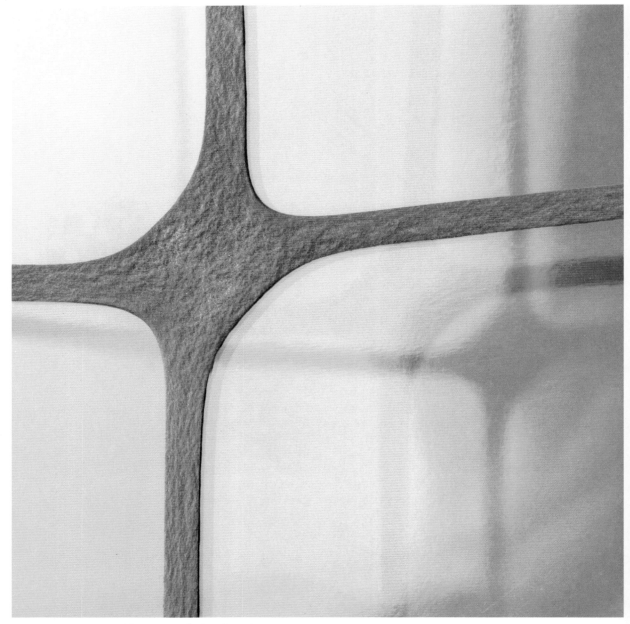

Unknown Designer
X-Band Rubber Bands, 1995
Synthetic rubber
Manufacturer: Mahakit Rubber Co., Thailand

Even objects that seem so spontaneous and uncomplicated as to defy all design control were instead carefully conceived. The nondescript rubber band,
for instance, was designed in London in 1845 by Stephen Perry, the owner of
a rubber manufacturing company. Perry's elastic was very similar to, and yet
also a far cry from this startling four-way version, all the more unexpected
because it is a radical mutation on one of the most established and incon-
spicuous objects in our world.

    The elastic band is the straightest application of Charles Goodyear's
1839 invention of the vulcanization process. Goodyear came across his discovery by accidentally dropping some rubber mixed with sulfur onto a hot
stove. His method made natural rubber impervious to weather conditions and
more elastic. The largest part of the rubber produced today is a synthetic de-
rivate of crude oil, rather than the original sap from trees. The rubber band,
without which life would be much more difficult, has absorbed all this
progress in its elastic memory.

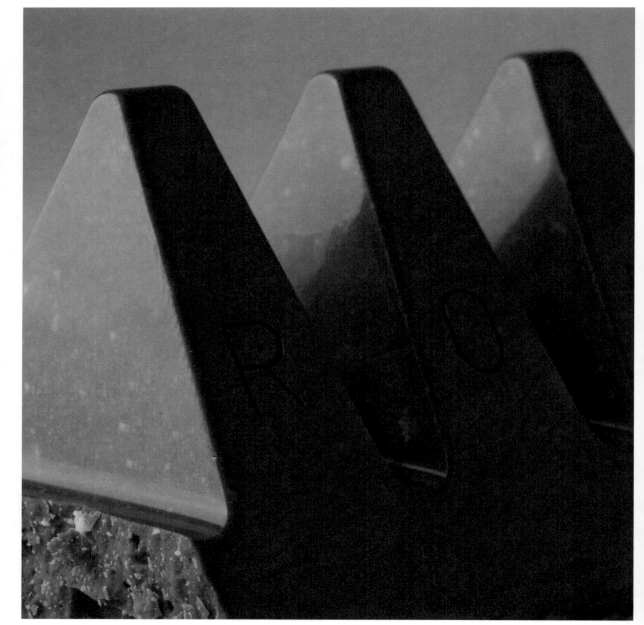

Theodor Tobler, Swiss, 1876–1941
Emil Baumann, Swiss, 1883–1966
Toblerone, 1908
Chocolate, honey, and almonds
Manufacturer: Fabrique de Chocolat Berne, Tobler & Cie., Switzerland;
now part of Kraft Foods Global, USA

In 1899, Johann Jakob Tobler, owner of a small confectionery business in Bern, Switzerland, founded his own chocolate factory together with his three sons. One of them, Theodor Tobler, and his cousin and production manager, Emil Baumann, began to experiment with the so-called Montelimar nougat that they had brought back from France in 1908. Eventually they settled on a mix of milk chocolate, honey, and almonds, the recipe of the Toblerone bar. In 1909 Toblerone was the first patented milk chocolate with almonds and honey, and thereafter the name, packaging, and triangular shape—its true symbol—also became registered brands. Toblerone is a wordplay on the names "Tobler," the firm name, and *torrone*, the Italian word for honey-almond nougat. There are two different explanations for the origin of the Toblerone bar's unique shape. It is commonly accepted that its triangular shape reflects that of the Matterhorn, one of the most famous mountains in the Swiss Alps, whose stylized image adorns the current triangular box. It is also rumored that on one of Tobler's frequent visits to the Folies Bergères in Paris, the human pyramid formed by the dancers onstage at the close of the show inspired the unconventional shape. Whatever its origin, the little mountains make the chocolate easy to share, fun to eat, and altogether unforgettable.

Tetra Pak Research Laboratories, Swedish, established 1951
Tetra Brik, 1959
Carton and plastic coating
Manufacturer: Tetra Pak, Sweden

In 1943, Ruben Rausing, a Swede who had been working on developing new types of packaging since 1930, began to research a new type of container that would solve the hygiene and fragility problems of glass bottles. By March 1944, Rausing had developed a tetrahedral container that formed a triangular package sealed by a strip along one side. The trick to the package was its airtightness, as the package was manufactured on a continuous basis out of a blank tube of paper that was folded and closed around a steady stream of liquid at regular intervals. The shape gave name to the company Tetra Pak, which was established in 1951 in Lund, Sweden. The Tetra Pak was officially launched in 1952, shortly after the first machine arrived at the new factory.

The original design, while remarkable in its inexpensiveness and airtight capabilities, proved difficult for the user to the point where one American dairy had to offer to pay for the dry cleaning bills customers suffered because of inadvertent spillage from the difficult-to-open paks. People had to use knives or scissors to open the containers, and the pressured contents tended to fly out immediately, spraying everything in the vicinity. In 1963, this problem was addressed with the launch of the Tetra Brik carton, the currently familiar six-sided rectangular box with a fold across the top and one across the bottom, and in 1977 the product was launched in the United States. The Tetra Brik still has to be opened using scissors, but the triangular piece created by the extra fold material proved much more manageable than the oddly shaped Tetra Pak. Production of Tetra Pak packages (including the Tetra Brik) currently exceeds sixty billion units.

Horoi Satoh, Japanese
Ping-Pong Paddle, 1952
This model: Tashika Penhold Racket
Wood and foam
Manufacturer: Butterfly, USA

In the nineteenth century, the members of the Victorian upper class loved to shake their crinolines by playing a makeshift sort of indoor tennis, using everyday objects as stand-ins for rackets, balls, and nets on common tables. In time, and presumably after a few domestic accidents, the amusement became more structured and was provided with specially produced equipment, manufactured at first by the American company Parker Brothers. The original paddles were built like tambourines, with parchment stretched onto a wooden frame.

The early years of the twentieth century saw a rapid fire of momentous events in the history of table tennis, from the British company J. Jacques & Son's copyright of the name "ping pong" in 1901, to James Gibb's introduction in England of celluloid balls he had found in the United States, not to mention the design of the first modern racket in 1902. It was E. C. Goode, also an Englishman, who first applied pebbled rubber to the wooden paddle, and his innovation lives on in the official rules of the game to this day. All official paddles must in fact be made of wood covered with rubber, with one side red, and the other one black.

A new innovation, nonetheless, made the paddles even more effective and comfortable to handle, and the game faster and more entertaining. The foam rubber paddle was launched by the Japanese Horoi Satoh in 1952.

Today's high-performance paddles can be made not only of wood, but also of graphite paired with sophisticated synthetic rubbers with exotic names.

Smart Design, American, established 1979
Good Grips Paring Knife, 1989
Stainless steel and synthetic rubber
Manufacturer: Oxo International, USA

Sam Farber, the founder of the American kitchenware company Copco in 1960 and nephew of the founder of Farberware, decided to devote his entrepreneurial experience to people with physical disabilities and impairments after his retirement from Copco in 1988. Prompted also by the arthritis that his wife Betsey had developed, which made cooking a painful chore as opposed to the pleasure it had always been, Farber decided in 1989 to do something about the problem. He called upon several design consultants and asked the New York–based office Smart Design to develop a new line of kitchen utensils. Oxo Good Grips was introduced in 1990.

The grip was indeed the focus of the design. Oval in shape and formed out of thermoplastic elastomer—a synthetic rubber that could be molded in detail by injection—the handle was outfitted with knife blades, can openers, and potato peelers. The gill-like incisions on the handle, in particular, made for a really good grip, but Oxo did not stop at that. Utensils that involved measures would provide very clear graphics and color markings for visibility. Tools that were previously designed in nonergonomic ways, for instance a cleaning brush that would require a torsion of the wrist, would be redesigned entirely—the brush to fit in the center of the palm of the hand. It was a whole new design philosophy, and the line that had been initially devised for a few has become favored by all for its beauty, comfort, and intelligence—a great example of universal design.

Hermann Steiner, Swiss, born 1913
Lamello Biscuit Joiner, 1955
Beech wood
Manufacturer: Steiner Lamello, Switzerland

Hermann Steiner was a Swiss engineer with a penchant for cabinetmaking. He opened a shop in 1944, and was intent on finding a way of using chipboard, recently introduced, to join various furniture parts together. He developed the biscuit joiner and called it by the name Lamello, which he derived from the German word *lamelle*, derived from Latin and meaning "thin plate."

The biscuit joiner is a wooden faceplate, egg-shaped and cut at a forty-five-degree angle with the wood grain, and etched on the surface in a regular pattern. The design of the plate provides both for maximum load spreading and for a better surface for glue to adhere. Currently, conventional biscuits are made from compressed and die-stamped beech and fit in cutouts created by a thin four-inch blade.

Steiner's Lamello was slow to catch on, and he was compelled to initiate a series of "my joint is stronger than your joint" challenges with fellow cabinetmakers, daring them to break joints set with his plate joiner. They were, of course, unable to, and the *lamelle* quickly caught on, although the original one designed by Steiner was then and remains now the most expensive version. The first stationary biscuit-joining machine appeared in 1956, while the Lamello was introduced in the mid- to late 1960s. By 1977, the biscuit joiner had been widely accepted as the strongest way to bond plates.

Klaus Gloger, Australian, n.d.
VarioPac Trigger Jewel Cases, 1992
Metallocene plastic
Manufacturer: VarioPac Systems Services, Germany

We have all expressed frustration at the roughness and brittleness of old-fashioned acrylic CD cases—also called "jewel boxes." But while most of us were simply content with voiced complaints, Klaus Gloger set out to do something definitive about it. His design, which was at first called Sonopak, was brought to reality by Heinz Diestelhorst, a German engineer with whom Gloger partnered shortly after getting his patent. Diestelhorst, with his extensive knowledge of plastics, contributed the smoothness and gentleness of the mechanism, not to mention the mesmerizing movement of the colorful trigger behind the milky white case.

The new type of polypropylene employed is completely recyclable and extremely strong. It is used to produce the entire system that has grown around Gloger's invention, which includes clips to add the discs to binders.

HUMBLE MASTERPIECES   / Pushpins

Edwin Moore, American, 1878–1916
Pushpins, 1900
This model: plastic and steel
Manufacturer: Moore Push-Pin Company, USA

Edwin Moore invented the pushpin because of his Princeton roommate, a photographer who needed help to post his films and plates to the wall. Moore, an inventive student, took to the chemistry lab and began experimenting, melting glass over a simple gas burner with a pair of pliers, and pushing an old phonograph needle into the resulting material to create the first version of the soon ubiquitous pushpin. His roommate liked it, as did others who Moore showed it to, who asked where they could get similar tacks. The seed of an entrepreneurial idea was planted, and Moore patented the pushpin in 1900, a year after he'd invented it. Legend has it that he made his glass push-pins by night and sold them by day, and while the length of time required for the glass to settle means that he couldn't have sold the very same pins he made the night before on the day after, it has remained company (and family) lore. Moore would still melt glass over equipment similar to a gas burner, ram the blunt end of a point into it, let it harden for three or four days, and sift through the pins, throwing away any that had cracked while hardening. As a next step, Moore devised a mold with a space for the pin to stand upright, a method the company he founded used for ten or fifteen years until semi-automation was developed in the 1920s, after Moore's 1916 death from the Philadelphia influenza epidemic.

In the 1950s the company started using plastic and aluminum, and the use of glass was discontinued shortly thereafter. By the 1960s the process was much more automated, and the Moore Push-Pin Company (still run by the family) produces seventy to eighty million pushpins a year.

Luigi D'Andrea, American, born Italy, 1886–1957
Guitar Pick, 1922
Celluloid
Manufacturer: D'Andrea, USA

The introduction of the polymer guitar pick not only improved rock stars' lives and careers but also saved the existence of the Atlantic hawksbill turtle, whose shell had been used to make picks for as long as people were pluck-ing on stringed instruments with something other than their fingers.

Tortoiseshell picks were made by soaking a shell in oil and pressing it between heated stainless steel plates that were regularly tightened, slowly and gradually straightening the irregularly shaped shell into something out of which rounded triangular picks could be stamped, tumbled, and hand-fin-ished. With John Wesley Hyatt's discovery of the semisynthetic celluloid in 1870, guitar picks began to be produced to a much larger scale in many dif-ferent patterns. The flexibility, thickness, and timbre of the celluloid were close enough to that of real tortoiseshell that the newer picks quickly caught on.

Legend has it that Luigi D'Andrea, a Naples-born vacuum cleaner sales-man, developed a method for manufacturing and marketing picks punched out of strips of celluloid in 1922. The coup came in the marketing, which his son Anthony took upon himself to do, eventually selling picks to the renowned music store G. Schirmer, which put the picks on the map. Currently there are about six main types of guitar picks. The standard shape, recognized by mu-sic aficionados and guitarists alike, accounts for 90 percent of the picks on the market, while the elliptical pick, slightly thicker than the standard and lightly curved, is popular among bass players. The jazz pick, shaped like the standard but smaller, and the teardrop, even smaller than the jazz, are fa-vored among jazz guitarists, while other shapes, including the diamond and heart, are just for kicks.

Thomas Adams, American, 1818–1905
Adams Chewing Gum, 1871
Sap from sapodilla tree
Manufacturer: Chicle Adams & Co., USA; now Cadbury Schweppes, UK

In 1848, American John Curtis invented the chewing gum, inspired by *chicle,* an ancient Mayan recipe made from the sap of sapodilla trees, also diffused among North American natives, who used spruce trees. In the middle of the nineteenth century, Curtis began selling flavored paraffin gum for chewing. In 1869, the deposed Mexican dictator General Antonio López de Santa Anna, who was living in exile in the United States at the Staten Island home of photographer Thomas Adams, introduced Adams to chicle and suggested experimenting further with it to develop a sellable product by mixing it with rubber. Adams's initial attempts, all geared toward producing automobile tires, failed. Adams was about to throw the remaining lot of chicle into the East River when he ran into a little girl asking for a penny's worth of paraffin in a drugstore at the corner of Chambers and Broadway in Manhattan. It occurred to Adams that he could make chewing gum out of the chicle, which would allow him to use up his stock. In February 1871, little sticks of pure chicle wrapped in colored tissue papers went on sale in New York drugstores under the name of "Adams New York Gum No. 1." They cost a penny apiece.

It wasn't until 1880, however, that gum became fully flavored. The welcome innovation is ascribed to William J. White, a popcorn salesman from Cleveland who eventually, in 1899, became president of the American Chicle Company, with Thomas Adams Jr. as chairman of the board of directors.

Ernö Rubik, Hungarian, born 1944
Rubik's Cube Puzzle, 1974
Plastic
Manufacturer: Ideal Toy Corporation, Hong Kong

The Rubik's Cube has become one of the most iconic designs in recent memory, but had its humble beginnings as a professor's study in geometry and three-dimensional forms. Its designer, Ernö Rubik, a lecturer at the Department of Interior Design at the Academy of Applied Arts and Crafts in Budapest, began visualizing his cube in 1974 but found constructing a working model to be more difficult than he'd initially anticipated. The cube, to him, presented a design problem: How could the blocks move independently without falling apart? Rubik developed a cylindrical interior, and found inspiration for the exterior mechanism in the smooth pebbles near the Danube. The final cube was made of twenty-six individual cubes, with each layer of nine twisting over a central axis, held together by the cube's unseen internal shape. Rubik hand-carved and assembled the cubes, marking each side with paper of a different color. He began twisting it, and was so excited by his mechanism working that he lost track of himself and couldn't figure out how to return the cubes to their original solid-sided formations. Rubik demonstrated the cube to his students and let friends play with it, only to find that everyone who tried it became completely obsessed. By 1979 cube enthusiasts could be found all over Hungary. But it was ultimately a mathematician's article appearing on the cover of *Scientific American* in 1979 that led to the cube's universal success, which continued until a 1983 crash of what had been a 100-million-cube fad. Recently, the cube has recaptured the public imagination and new versions, for instance four-by-four-inch instead of the three-by-three-inch cubes, have joined the family.

There is only one correct answer—and forty-three quintillion wrong ones—when solving the three-by-three-inch Rubik's Cube. No one has solved the puzzle in fewer than fifty-two moves.

PAOLA ANTONELLI

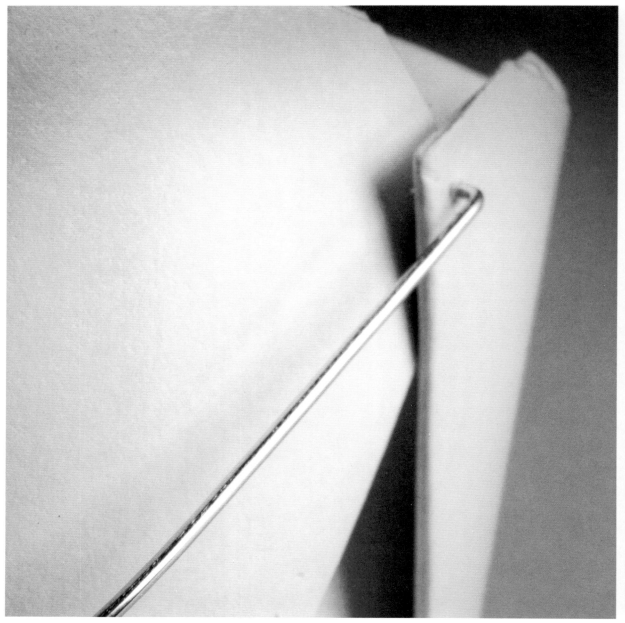

Unknown Designer
Chinese Take-out Box, n.d.
Paper with plastic coating, metal

Here's to another great design icon, the box for take-out Chinese food. Leakproof and elegant in its simplicity, this folded paper vessel has inspired high-end fashion designers, who have reproduced it in satin and velvet, and schoolchildren alike. Made from a single sheet of coated cardboard and a measure of thin wire for a handle and a lock, the box comes in several different sizes and can safely contain sauces and semiliquid foods, as well as noodles and rice. Moreover, the box is perfect to eat directly from, especially when using chopsticks.

Mysteriously, no information could be found about the invention and the history of this ubiquitous and ingenious object. Nevertheless, this collection of humble masterpieces would not have been the same without it.

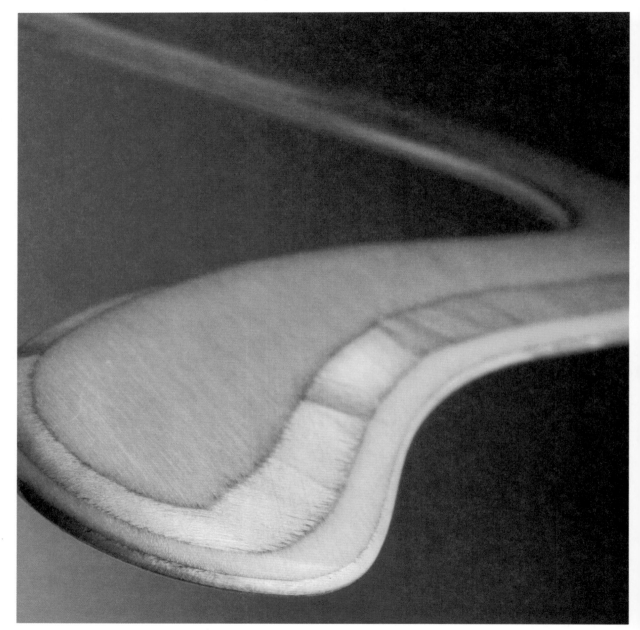

Unknown Designer, Aboriginal
Boomerang, 15,000 years ago
Wood

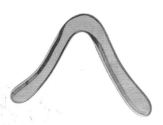

The boomerang begins as a hunting stick used by ancient people to stun, par-
alyze, or kill animals. An original version, referred to in Australia as the *kylie,*
was a heavy non-returning aerodynamic stick, thrown horizontally the way the
returning boomerang is now. A throwing stick carbon-dated at over twenty-
thousand years old was discovered in what is now Poland, and King Tutankhamen, the prolific ancient Egyptian collector, is said to have owned a
substantial boomerang collection.

Australian Aborigines, who interestingly never developed the use of the
bow and arrow for hunting or protection, are widely credited with discovering
the returning properties of a tweaked version of the kylie. Boomerangs are
slightly thinner, lighter, and more important, more curved than non-returning sticks. Their name comes from the Turuwal people of New South Wales.

Boomerangs were used for fun for years, but the organized sport began
in the 1960s, with its popularity triggered by a 1968 *Scientific American* article.
The United States Boomerang Association was formed in 1980, and the sport
Twenty-five countries have national boomerang organizations, and there are
currently hundreds of shapes of boomerangs. The three most common ones
are a three-winged version (for beginners), the familiar wishbone shape (for
advanced throwers), and a trimmed-down iteration of the wishbone, for the
competitive boomerang player.

Daniel F. Cudzik, American, born 1934
Beverage Can with Non-removable Pull-Tab Opener—Stay-on Tab, 1975
Aluminum
Manufacturer: Alcoa, USA

Before Daniel Cudzik invented the stay-on metal tab in the 1960s (patenting it in 1975), tabs from metal cans were ripped off and thrown away, littering sidewalks, streets, and beaches. Today, every single one of the billion-plus cans manufactured per year features Daniel Cudzik's tab. No more cut feet, no more litter, and best of all, no one ever has to think about where to throw that pesky tab.

The metal can, first developed by Frenchman Nicolas Appert in response to Napoleon's challenge to come up with a way of storing food for his troops, and later patented by Englishman Peter Durand in the early nineteenth century, underwent many changes in the attempt to find the right material, perfect the design, and simplify the manufacturing process. The first can in aluminum with an easy-open end and a pull ring was introduced in 1961, and at that time, companies were studying the possibility of adding plastics to the design in order to improve it. Cudzik, a tools developer employed by can manufacturer Reynolds Metal, insisted on working with the original aluminum, because attaching plastic to the cans—which were banged out of a sheet of metal every fifth of a second—added far too much time and complexity. The idea hit him while he was watching TV with his two children, aged seven and eight. He sketched a proposal for both the tab itself and the machinery it would require, gave it to a draftsman to draw at ten times the size (creating a 36-foot-long blueprint), and built a mock-up out of cardboard, aluminum foil, and tape. The prototype worked.

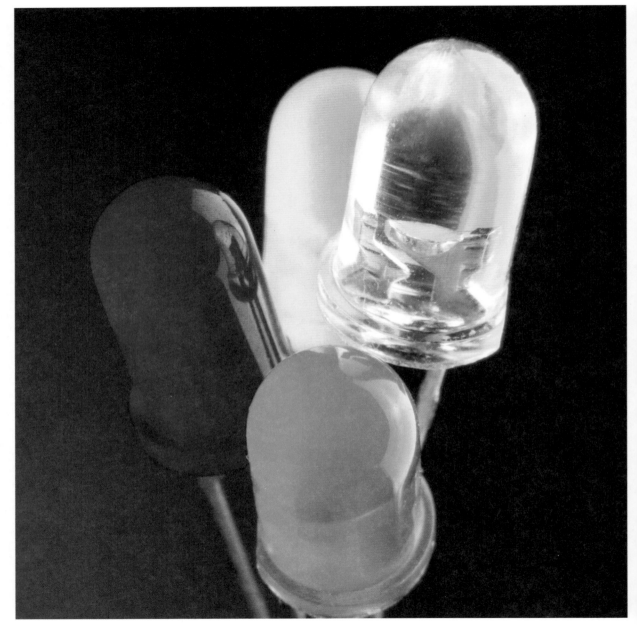

Nick Holonyak, American, born 1928
Light-Emitting Diode (LED), 1962
Various materials

Dr. Nick Holonyak, who liked to exercise by walking across the floor on his hands and climbing twenty-foot ropes, invented the very first light-emitting diode (LED for short) in 1962, while he was employed by General Electric. A student of one of the transistor's inventors, John Bardeen, Holonyak had decided to concentrate on silicon and in particular on the study of semiconductors.

LEDs, ubiquitous today in objects ranging from traffic lights and signs to television screens, watches, and remote controls, are tiny lightbulbs without a filament. They fit easily onto wires and in an electrical circuit and are illuminated by the movement of the electrons in a semiconducting material. The popular market for them exploded in the late 1960s, when all at once several companies began seeing potential applications of red LEDs, the first type to be developed, in the display of devices from the calculator to the wristwatch.

Once the potential of the red LED had been exhausted, newer colors began to be developed through the ingenious application of various gases. Yellow was the first new color, shortly followed by an improved version of the original red, after which green, orange, and then high-brightness red were developed. Today, LEDs can be found where exceptional brightness and dependability are needed, for instance in traffic lights, as well as in some innovative car lights.

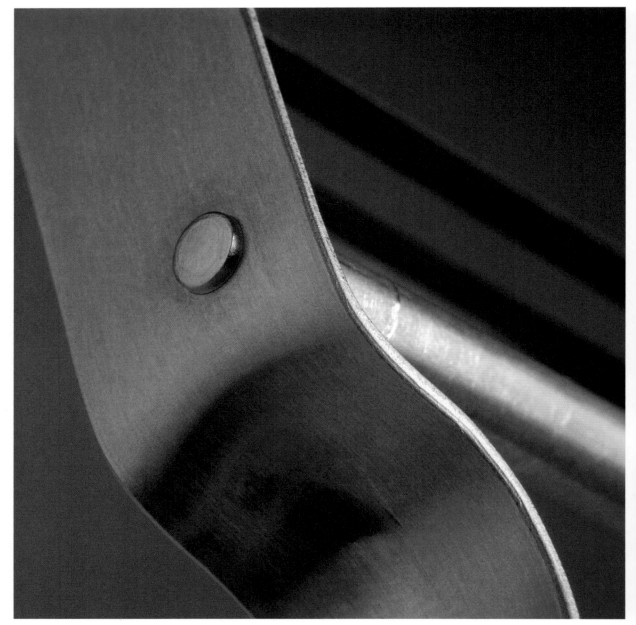

Alfred Neweczeral, Swiss, 1899–1958
Rex Potato Peeler, 1947
Aluminum and steel
Manufacturer: Zena, Switzerland

The Rex potato peeler, the ubiquitous kitchen utensil, which was commemorated in 2003 by its native country with a stamp, was designed in 1947 by inventor Alfred Neweczeral, the son of Prussian immigrants. A U-shaped aluminum bow, the lightweight Rex potato peeler was designed with both left- and right-handed users in mind.

The cutter head is made of moveable stainless steel, strong enough to scoop out potato eyes. The head also stops the blade from cutting too far into the potato, guarding against waste of what was at the time of invention a supremely valuable food. The horizontal blade makes for easy peeling by allowing the user to peel away without having to skew the wrist into uncomfortable positions, and the overall light weight and easy shape allow it to fit comfortably into the entire hand. Neweczeral founded Zena AG in Switzerland, which continues to manufacture and sell the original potato peeler. The design is internationally protected, and the peeler has received several awards for its intelligence and beauty.

Unknown Designer, Chinese
Folding Fan, eighteenth century

The use of personal fans dates back as far as the reign of Egypt's King Tutankhamen, while its uses have encompassed both the obvious cooling and the more secretive art of fan-based flirtation in the heavily supervised social life of the nineteenth century.

Early fans were typically made of feathers, woven reeds, bamboo, paper, silk, or parchment, and were flat discs until the beginning of the eighteenth century, when the foldable fan, first developed on the coasts of China and Japan, was introduced in Europe. Both the construction and the application of fans were elevated to an art form, with fans variously painted, embroidered, and handled for function, fun, and social communication. In the nineteenth century, the sophisticated and witty British prime minister Benjamin Disraeli denounced the fans as doing more damage than swords because of the class-consciousness and jealousy the different types of fans invited, while the clergy deemed them just plain wicked. By that time, the art of the fan had taken on an incredibly complex code, called *abanico*, meaning "fan" in Spanish. Girls who were otherwise beset at every move by watchers making sure they didn't dally with the wrong suitor were able to communicate messages, from "I will marry you" and "We are just friends" to the much more complex "You've treated me infernally" all the way through "I'm thinking about whether our re-lationship is convenient," the last one communicated by touching the fan to the palm of the hand. While this language, like many others, has today sadly been lost, foldable fans, in their simplicity and functionality, are making a slow and persistent comeback.

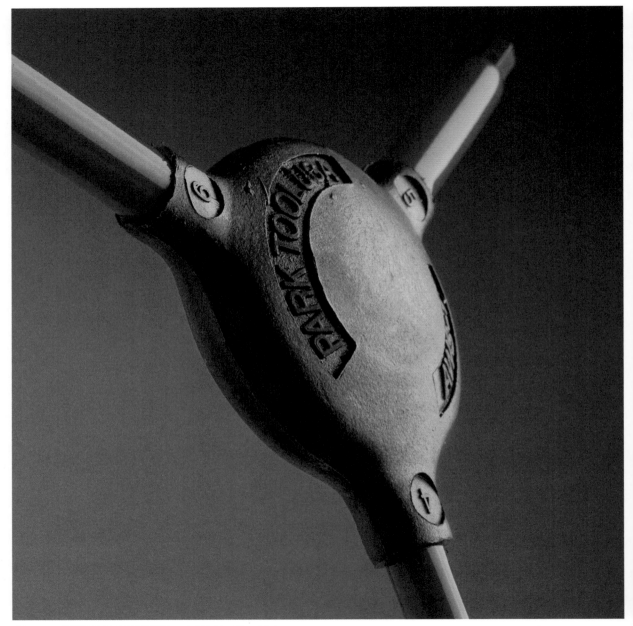

Howard Hawkins, American, born 1932
Eric Hawkins, American, born 1962
AWS-1 Hex Wrench Set, 1984
Nylon and steel
Manufacturer: Park Tool Co., USA

The first three-sided wrench with hexagonal heads was developed in 1984 as
a response to the growing need for something to fix bikes that was quick,
efficient, and easy to store. Allen bolts—the bolts with hexagonal holes used
to adjust handlebars, saddles, and accessories on most bicycles—come in
three sizes, all accommodated by this compact tool. More important, the
shape of the wrench itself makes it much easier to use and much more efficient. The Y shape improves leverage, making the wrench also easier for
users with a weaker grip.

Designed by Eric Hawkins and his father Howard, the shape was
achieved by the two just playing around with tool pieces and pressing the
wrench bits into aluminum. In 1994, after ten years of this manufacturing
method and finding that it was difficult to keep the supply up to the ninety
thousand per year demand, they started manufacturing the wrench through
injection molding. According to Eric Hawkins, every mechanic currently uses
the wrench, and it's referred to simply as a "three-way."

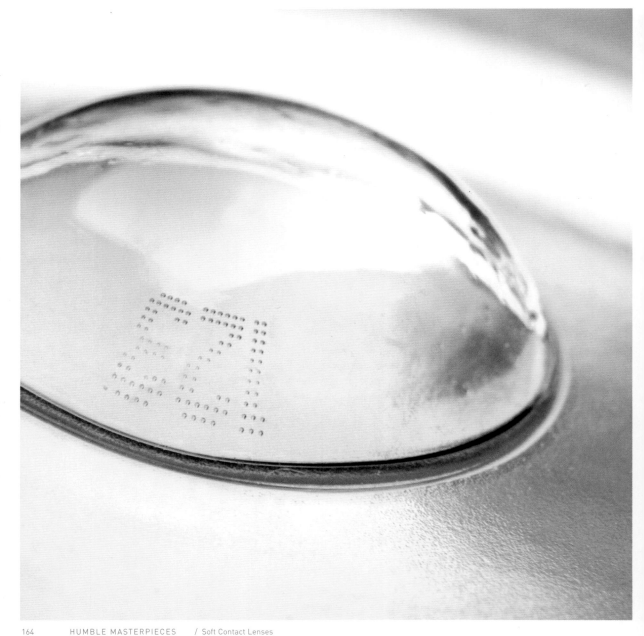

Otto Wichterle, Czechoslovakian, 1913–1998
Soft Contact Lenses, 1950s
Hydroxyethylmethacrylate plastic
This model manufactured by Bausch & Lomb, USA

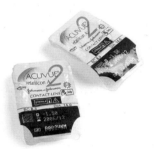

The invention of the contact lens begins, as do so many inventions, with Leonardo da Vinci, who sketched an idea for a contact lens in 1508. In the nineteenth century, scientists from all over the world developed eye coverings and various methods of grinding hard glass lenses to fit exactly to the eye's surface, and in 1929, Hungarian Joseph Dallos began taking molds directly from eyes. In 1936, New York optometrist William Feinbloom opened the door to soft contacts by making contact lenses out of plastic. In 1945, the American Optometric Association formally recognized contact lens development as a field, and in 1950 an Oregon optometrist designed a corneal lens, the inner surface of which followed the eye's shape.

These were all steps in the right direction, but it took Otto Wichterle, a chemical engineer, to fully develop a workable soft contact. Wichterle was working on nylon plastics when, legend has it, he saw a man on a train reading a magazine about ophthalmology, and realized that his recently developed water-swelling plastic gels could be used for eye care. It took him years (and painful self-tests) to develop a workable lens, and around Christmas of 1961 he produced his first prototypes. He tested them out on patients at a local hospital, who, to his delight, found no irritation, but unfortunately couldn't see any better, either. On New Year's of 1962, Wichterle teamed up with George Nissel, a hard contact lens maker. Together, they developed the idea of turning plastic on a lathe before it swelled, shaping the lens earlier. Wichterle licensed his technology in 1964.

Flaminaire, company design, French, established 1939
J1 Bic Disposable Lighter, 1972
Steel and Delrin plastic
Manufacturer: Société Bic, France

In 1971, the ballpoint company Bic acquired the French lighter company Flaminaire, known for producing high-quality (and long-lasting) handheld lighters. Bic saw beyond the permanent keepsake lighter, a category that also included that other pillar of the history of design, the robust Zippo, (see page 205) and devised a lighter that was at once disposable and stylish for the days, weeks, or (optimistically) months that a smoker would carry it. A group of engineers worked for a few months on a disposable gas lighter, trying to develop something that was more elegant and, crucially, stronger than the competition's attempts. A first prototype was developed that seemed to work until someone cracked the lighter by pressing the spark wheel too hard in the middle of a test ignition. Marcel Bich, head of the Bic company, was unhappy with this crack, and set the team back to work to develop a virtually unbreakable lighter. The final product is an engineering marvel, much like the Bic pen and disposable razor that would complete the classic range of the company.

One of the new lighter's defining features was its comfortable oval section. While Bic insisted that everything be manufactured to the highest level, it was the shape that set the lighter apart from its contemporary competitors. In 1973, a first lighter with an adjustable flame was launched in many colors, and over the coming years, new versions of the classic were introduced, including a mini version in 1985 and a decorated version in 1990.

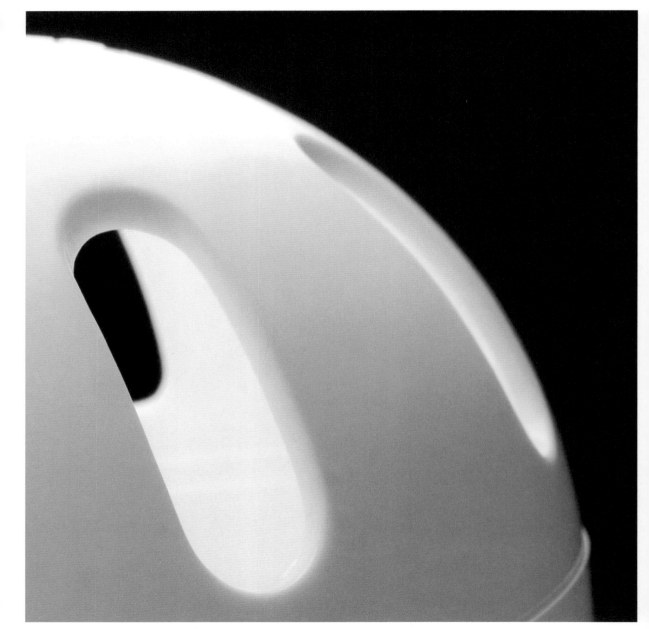

HUMBLE MASTERPIECES / Wiffle Ball

David N. Mullany, American, 1908–1990
David A. Mullany, American, born 1940
Wiffle Ball, 1953
Polyethylene plastic
Manufacturer: The Wiffle Ball, USA

The Wiffle Ball, an exquisite invention that has delighted generations of Americans, turned fifty in 2003. As happens with many design masterpieces, it was born out of a haphazard moment of acute observation. Legend has it that one evening of 1953, David N. Mullany of Shelton, Connecticut, on the way home from work paused to look at his teenage son playing baseball with his friends in the backyard. They were using a golf ball and a broomstick and with such rudimentary tools, as kids always do, they were trying to mimic one of baseball's most heroic feats, the curveball. The curveball became the focus of Mullany's design breakthrough: by making a ball whose two hemispheres were different in weight, he reasoned, he could induce the special effect. A friend working in a nearby factory provided him with samples of a round plastic gift box that had been made for Coty, the perfume house, and his first step was to cut away material from one half of the sphere. As it turned out, not only the subtraction of weight, but also the shape of the cuts was crucial.

Mullany so believed in his Wiffle ball—named after "whiff," the term children used to mock batters who missed—that he invested everything he had in his new company. The ball, beloved by parents for the way it allows kids to throw balls without breaking windows, and by kids because it reduces disparity by making the game more dependent on skills than on weight and strength, is still manufactured in the family, by Mullany's son and his grandsons, in a small factory near New Haven, Connecticut.

John Walker, British, 1771–1859
Friction Match, 1826
Wood, sulfur, and phosphorus

In this humblest of objects lies a power that humankind had been seeking to perfect for centuries: a way to have control over fire. It took centuries of fine-tuning and trial and error, with the latest steps before 1826 involving mainly white phosphorus—extremely inflammable when in contact with air—and sulfur in various combinations, to get to the first stable mixture and the first box of matches sold in 1827. In 1845, a red form of phosphorus took over the market, and around 1855 it was used in the so-called safety match, a match-cum-box combination that safely split the igniting process between the match and the container.

However, most of the phosphorus combinations used until that moment were highly poisonous, provoking grave diseases among the factory workers and fatal consequences for children who sucked on the matches by mistake. Matches were so dangerous that by the 1870s they were nicknamed "lucifers." In 1910, however, the Diamond Match Company at last deposited a patent for a nonpoisonous phosphorus compound. The innovation proved so universally important that President William H. Taft asked the company to surrender the patent, so that it could be used widely. Diamond did, in a rare gesture of corporate generosity.

Today, 500 billion matches are used each year.

Anthony Maglica, American, born 1930
Mini Maglite, 1987
Aluminum
Manufacturer: Mag Instrument, USA

The era of the single flashlight kept in the garage or under the bed, with the user knowing it'll work regardless of how many times it's been used before, was ushered in only with the introduction of Anthony Maglica's Maglite. Until he came along and introduced his idea, the flashlight was an unreliable item, typically thrown away once it had quickly worn itself out.

Anthony Maglica was born in New York City and raised in Croatia. He returned to the United States in 1950 in order to take advantage of the free enterprise dream offered to so many immigrants, and settled down in California. Learning a few words of English every day and saving up money by working odd jobs, he came up with enough to put a $125 down payment on a lathe, which he used to start Mag Instrument in his garage in Los Angeles. Initially, Maglica produced machine tools for industry use and soon earned acclaim as an industrial, aerospace, and military machine parts manufacturer. Seeing a niche for a sturdy flashlight, he developed the Maglite flashlight in 1979, targeting it at firefighters and policemen, who were definite clients for such a reliable product. In 1982, Maglica, along with the eighty employees he had amassed at that point, moved into a huge facility in southern California and introduced the rechargeable flashlight system, the most powerful rechargeable flashlight of its size on the market. In 1984, a smaller rechargeable Maglite was introduced, and in 1987, the triple-A battery-size Mini Maglite entered the market. In 1988, in a turn back to the old days, a tiny Solitaire Maglite was developed. All product and research development is still done by Anthony Maglica himself.

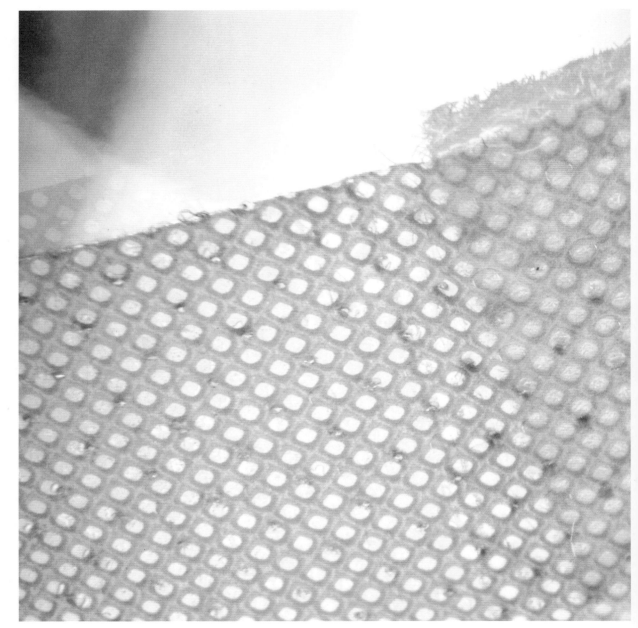

Earle Dickson, American, 1891–1936
Band-Aid, 1921
Adhesive bandage and cotton
Manufacturer: Johnson & Johnson, USA

Earle Dickson, a cotton buyer at Johnson & Johnson, lived in New Brunswick, New Jersey, with his young wife, Josephine, who was prone to cutting and burning her fingers while preparing food. Therefore, he decided to prepare some ready-made bandages to make it easier for her to cover and protect her cuts. He took squares of cotton gauze and placed them at intervals along an adhesive strip, and covered the cotton with crinoline to keep it sterile. When Earle told his boss about his invention, James Johnson decided to manufacture the adhesive bandages and sell them to the public under the famous Band-Aid trademark. Earle was soon nominated vice president of the company.

The Band-Aid brand has become an almost generic name, so ubiquitous is its use. To this day, more than one hundred billion Band-Aid adhesive bandages have been made, in several varieties and sizes, from the decorated ones—first introduced in 1956—to the ones pretreated with antibiotics.

Unknown Designer
Flip-Flop's, late 1940s
Rubber and plastic
This model manufactured by Havaianas, Brazil

The sturdy yet disposable flip-flop, the choice of boys, girls, men, and women everywhere who want to wear something quick, light, and easy on their feet, was introduced to North America only after World War II, following short on the heels of a long Japanese history.

The flip-flop's shape is inspired by the traditional Japanese *zori*, a flat-bottomed open sandal with just a thong of material between the big and second toes to keep it in place. The *zori* was itself a riff on the original *geta*, an elevated wooden platform with two cloth straps that formed a V, which women wore to ensure that their kimonos did not drag in the mud. While the sandal had caught on all over Asia, its diffusion in the Western world began in Hawaii in the aftermath of World War II, hence the nickname *havaianas* used in many countries, such as Brazil. A shortage of manufacturing materials in time of war made the flip-flop, in its simplicity and sparseness, very appropriate. California surfers adopted them immediately.

Anecdotes surrounding the flip-flop include one describing the way in which Japanese authorities distinguished Koreans living in Japan from native Japanese in the 1950s. Apparently, only the Japanese had been wearing *zori* sandals long enough to have developed a big space between their big and second toes, which questioning authorities latched onto as a definitive marker of race. A documented cultural difference is one between the way Americans and Japanese wear flip-flops, American men gripping the sandal tightly at the V, while the Japanese drag their heels and primarily use their thigh muscles.

Sven Wingquist, Swedish, 1876–1953
Self-Aligning Ball Bearing, 1907
Chrome-plated steel
Manufacturer: SKF Industries, USA

Both efficient and beautiful, the ball bearing can be seen as an emblem of the machine age—a name often used to define the 1920s and 1930s, when industrial designers as well as consumers not only took a new interest in the look and style of commercial products, but also delighted themselves in considering machinery parts objects of pure functional beauty, a celebration of the new era of mechanical production.

Ball bearings are indeed a fundamental element of mechanical production. Without them, there would be a constant need to replace parts worn out by friction. With them, machine parts gently slide on each other with greatly reduced wear. The most immediate representation of this concept are roller skates, whose wheels are nothing more than ball bearings padded by wood or resin, the steel balls bearing the load of the body, allowing the wheels to spin smoothly.

Philip Vaughan invented the original ball bearing in England in 1794, but Winquist's design represents a radical departure from what was available in the nineteenth century. This sturdy steel ball bearing is composed of a double layer of balls in a race. This type of bearing was structurally superior to the sliding bearing, which has only one line of balls and which wastes some energy in realigning machinery shafts thrown off during assembly-line manufacturing. The self-aligning quality of the ball bearing made it a superior product, since the bearing could absorb some shaft misalignment without lowering its endurance. More important, it solved the problem of overheating, making industrial production processes all over the world more efficient.

Godtfred Kirk Christiansen, Danish, 1920–1995
LEGO Building Bricks, 1954–1958
ABS plastic
Manufacturer: LEGO Group, Denmark

It was 1932 when Ole Kirk Christiansen founded a small carpentry business in the village of Billund and dedicated most of his time to building toys, and 1934 when he came up with the name that made his business famous. In Danish, *leg godt* means "play well"—while in Latin, *lego* means "I learn"—and for several decades the LEGO Building Bricks have inspired children all around the world to do exactly that.

In 1949, Christiansen developed his wooden Automatic Binding Bricks, renamed LEGO Bricks in 1954. The current plastic bricks, with their stud-and-tube coupling system, were introduced in 1958 and imported into the United States in 1962. These bricks were made of cellulose acetate and later replaced with acrylonitrile butadiene styrene (ABS), a more stable plastic with better color quality. These miniature modular pieces came in various colors, shapes, and sizes and enabled kids to construct cars, buildings, pirate ships, spacecrafts, and many three-dimensional play environments. Godtfred Kirk Christiansen, the founder's son, believed that play is a process of learning and discovery and that these were essential components of a child's development.

Recent developments include interactive software, a story-driven building universe, and robotics programming and construction. LEGO has even developed a business-strategy building system for adults called LEGO Serious Play. LEGO estimates that over the past sixty years, its global sales translate into the equivalent of fifty-two blocks for each of the world's six billion inhabitants.

Earle Cleveland Haas, American, 1888–1981
Tampax, 1929
Cotton, paper
Manufacturer: Procter & Gamble, USA

Because of its extraordinary impact on the quality of life of women around the world, the sanitary tampon basks in the glow of significance and necessity, two of the characteristics of great design.

In 1929, Denver physician Dr. Earle Cleveland Haas spent much of his spare time developing the tampon in response to his wife's complaints about the discomfort she felt when wearing bulky pads. A friend happened to mention to him that she used a piece of sponge internally, which led him to speculate on the possibility of an internal control solution. He realized that compressed cotton had the same absorbent abilities as the described sponge, and developed a prototype in his basement, starting with strips of cotton two inches wide and five or six inches long and binding them together with a cord, leaving a little extra length for easy removal.

The kicker was the design of the telescopic paper applicator, which was not only practical and easy, but also flushable. When Tampax Incorporated (whose name alluded to its main product) was formally chartered in 1936, the trying task of marketing the new design began. The company hired educators they called "Tampax ladies" to dispel myths about the tampon, but it took an approving 1945 report by the *Journal of the American Medical Association* to bring them fully into the acceptable realm.

In World War II, the Tampax company was put at the lowest priority for receiving cotton rations, but managed to keep receiving them because less cotton was needed to manufacture tampons than the bulkier pads. The ad campaign that's still more or less in place, advertising the tampon's stealth when the wearer engages in physical activity, was fully developed during the war, when women were called to work as much as men were. The slogan, "No time for a time out," proved apt, and lasting.

Unknown Designer
Chopsticks, ca. 3,000 BC
Bamboo and wood

Developed approximately five thousand years ago, chopsticks were recorded in the Chinese *Book of Rites*, which describes Chinese religious practices from the eighth to the fifth century BC, as first having been used in the Shang Dynasty (1766–1121 BC). According to legend, chopsticks were developed by Yu (no last name necessary), an ancient Chinese tribe leader. The legend tells that Yu was so enveloped by his work that he had to eat more quickly than anyone else. Rather than wait for his food to be taken out of the communal cooking pot (which would allow it to cool), Yu was so intent on eating quickly that he would snap a twig into two pieces and use the resulting crude chopsticks to fish pieces of food out of the boiling water.

There are five types of chopsticks. Today, bamboo or wood utensils are most commonly used in homes and restaurants around the world, but chopsticks are also made out of metal, bone, stone, or a compound. Gold and silver chopsticks were used in the Tang Dynasty (AD 618–907), as it was believed that silver chopsticks could detect poisons lurking in meals. Research into the use of chopsticks has determined that more than thirty joints and fifty muscles are involved, which makes sense since the chopsticks act as extensions of fingers, applying the principle of the lever. The longest recorded chopsticks in the world reach nearly 40 centimeters, or 1⅓ feet. China currently produces more than 45 billion pairs of disposable chopsticks per year, while Japan produces around 25 billion.

Philips Research Laboratories, Dutch, established 1891
Sony Research Laboratories, Japanese, established 1946
Digital Compact Disc, 1970s
Polycarbonate plastic
Manufacturer: Royal Philips Electronics, the Netherlands

American engineer James T. Russell presented the first prototype of a CD in the late 1960s. Russell, who had worked at General Electric, loved to listen to music. In his quest for a better sound quality than that afforded by vinyl records, he first tried to replace his gramophone's stylus with a cactus needle, but found the hand sharpening necessary after each use slightly inconvenient. He worked on a system that would record and replay the music without physical contact between any of the elements, and realized that by using light he could store massive amounts of information on a small surface. He patented the first digital-optical recording and playback system in 1970, recording micron-diameter bits of light and darkness onto a photosensitive platter whose patterns were read by a laser, whose patterns were in turn read by a computer that converted the signal to an audible or visible transmission.

Meanwhile, in 1969, Dutch physicists Klaas Compaan and Piet Kramer started developing a system to record holographic images on a disc. In collaboration with Lou Ottens of Philips, who had previously worked on the compact audiocassette, they agreed on a polycarbonate disc with a diameter of 115 mm and presented a prototype in 1979. Needing a technology that Sony had already perfected, Philips struck a collaboration with the Japanese company that enabled them both to set the standards. The collaboration ended in 1981, and each company released its own CD players—and in Sony's case, also the first music CD, Billy Joel's *52nd Street*—as early as 1982.

Unknown Designer
Mascara Wand, 1960s
This model: Wand from Great Lash mascara, 1971
Manufacturer: Maybelline, USA

Like many other products in this book, mascara's origins hark back to the dawn of time. The name comes from the Arabic word for buffoon, *maskhara*, also the root of the word "mask." The cosmetic darkening of the eyes and eyelashes is celebrated in innumerable depictions of life starting in ancient Egypt and India, where the most diverse organic and inorganic matters—from honey to crocodile dung, lead, beeswax, and oil—were mixed to produce a paste. In 1917, T. L. Williams, inspired by his sister Mabel's use of petroleum jelly on her lashes, mixed it with coal dust and introduced the first commercial product, Maybelline, a combination of his sister's name and Vaseline's. It was sold as a cake that needed wetting to be applied with a brush.

The object of our attention is the packaging revolution that did away with the cake-and-water muddle. The first patent for a solution that integrated reservoir and applicator was awarded to a Frank L. Engel Jr. of Chicago in 1939. The war slowed down its advent on the market, and it was not until 1958 that Helena Rubinstein, a doyenne of the American cosmetics industry, introduced the aptly named Mascaramatic, a small, easy, and portable penlike reservoir whose cap was outfitted with a tip of grooved metal. With the introduction of numerous synthetic materials in the 1960s and the entry into the market of several international companies seeking to outperform one another with technology, the metal tip soon became a (magic) wand. The wands come today in different shapes, fine-tuned to the different effects—lengthening, thickening, curving—that the mascara promises to deliver. Shown here is the wand from Maybelline's classic Great Lash mascara, in homage to the early twentieth century innovation.

Chuck Hoberman, American, born 1956
Transforming Sphere, 1995
Polypropylene and ABS plastics
Manufacturer: Hoberman Designs, USA

In some fortunate cases, engineers become universal donors to a world
thirsty for new ideas and shapes. In the tradition of Buckminster Fuller,
whose work has inspired a variety of applications that range from architecture to the classic design for the soccer ball, Chuck Hoberman, an artist and
engineer, has devoted his life to collapsible and expandable structures. The
Transforming Sphere is his most renowned design. The original sphere, made
of aluminum, was installed in 1992 in the atrium of the Liberty Science Center
in Jersey City, New Jersey. A permanent kinetic sculpture, the sphere ex-
pands and contracts between 4.5 and 18 feet. Its toy version comes in four different sizes and was first manufactured in 1995. In his parallel life as a
structural engineer, Hoberman's most recent works include the arch that
was the centerpiece of Salt Lake City's 2002 Olympic Games.

William Middlebrook, American, n.d.
Gem Manufacturing Company, British, n.d.
Slide-on Paper Clip, 1890
Steel
This model manufactured by: ACCO Brands, USA

In the thirteenth century, long before the invention of the paper clip, people used to cut holes in the corners of pages and fasten them together with ribbons. The only development in paper fastening for six hundred years was to wax the ribbons to make them stronger. The modern paper clip, whose invention had to wait for the development of elastic steel wire, has been attributed to among others the Norwegian patent clerk Johann Vaaler, who invented a prototypical triangular paper clip and received a German patent in 1899, and the British Gem Manufacturing Company, which invented it as early as 1890, but obtained a patent only in 1907. It was the Gem Manufacturing Company that designed the first double oval shaped paper clip that is still in use today. William Middlebrook patented a machine for mass-producing Gem paper clips in 1899.

The paper clip is constantly being reinvented and improved upon, but it is a set of eight qualities that every paper clip strives for and that none has yet attained in unison. The paper clip should not catch, mutilate, or tear papers. It should not tangle with other clips, and should be able to hold a thick set of papers securely. A thin paper clip is ideal, since it takes up less space in files, requires less postage for sent document stacks, and uses less wire, keeping it cheap. It should be easily used. While no paper clip has yet achieved all eight qualities, it is one of the easiest to use and most enduring products ever designed, and shows no signs of being replaced. We might be using paper clips for the next six hundred years.

Olof Bäckström, Finnish, born 1922
O Series Scissors, 1960
ABS plastic and stainless steel
Manufacturer: Fiskars, Finland

How obvious, and yet how ingenious to design scissors with different size handles, to accommodate the way our hand will hold them! Often, the best examples of design come from the observation of how we truly use things, and craftsmen working with textiles had already used scissors of that kind for a long time. It was Fiskars's destiny to bring this common sense into the industrial era and to a wide audience. Olaf Bäckström, a Finnish engineer turned woodcarver, found a job as an industrial designer for Fiskars in 1958. After his first assignment, a successful line of tableware, he turned his attention to the scissors and shears that would later on make the Fiskars brand famous all over the world—and that would be copied ad infinitum. His sculptural habit with wood is somehow visible in the smooth, almost hand-carved quality of the handles, which would later on be produced by injection-molding in a completely automated process.

John Bardeen, American, 1908–1991
Walter H. Brattain, American, 1902–1987
William B. Shockley, American, 1910–1989
Transistor, 1947
Manufacturer: Bell Telephone Laboratories, USA

Before the invention of the transistor, which can be used analogically to amplify a signal for radio communication or digitally to open and close a circuit in a computer processor, people relied on an amplifying vacuum tube developed by eccentric inventor Lee de Forest in 1906, which was undependable, used too much power, and produced too much heat. At the end of World War II, Mervin Kelly, director of research for Bell Telephone Laboratories, put together a crack team of scientists, hoping that they could come up with something far better. Theoretician Bill Shockley was selected as team leader, while experimental physicist Walter Brattain and theoretical physicist John Bardeen rounded out the eclectic group.

Brattain and Bardeen made slow progress until, in the fall of 1946, Brattain dunked their entire setup in a water bucket in the laboratory, out of exasperation, frustration, or sheer inspiration. Bardeen realized that they'd been taking the wrong approach and had misunderstood the properties of electrons, and the two built a point-contact transistor made of a gold foil strip on a plastic triangle. Shockley was so disappointed by their scientific strides that he locked himself in a hotel room in Chicago and developed an idea on paper within four weeks—and a prototype within two years. The transistor was unveiled in 1948, and according to legend, was named with the help of a Bell Labs engineer who wrote science fiction in his spare time.

The three original scientists earned very little money from their research, but were honored with a Nobel Prize in 1956, once the impact of the transistor—which allowed journalist Charles Stewart to hear about the Martin Luther King assassination from a Bedouin tribesman listening to a transistor radio—was accepted. Today transistors are found in devices such as video cameras, cell phones, copy machines, cars, and video games. Without transistors, there would be no Internet and no space travel.

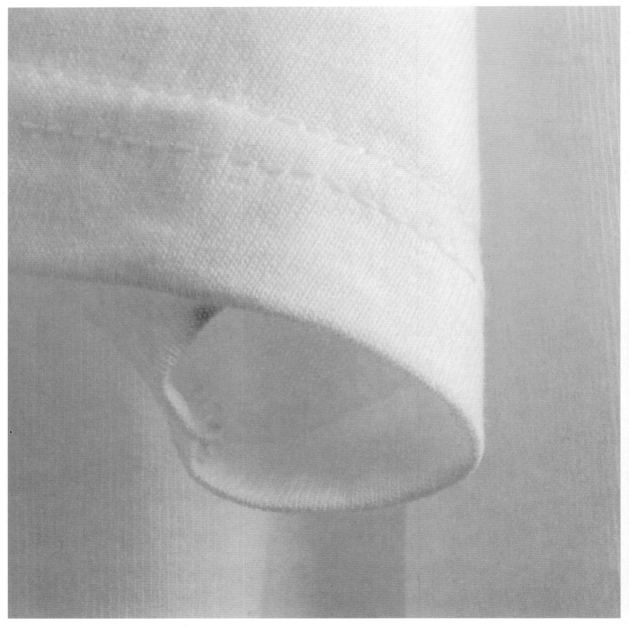

Unknown Designer
T-shirt, 1910s
Cotton
This model manufactured by Fruit of the Loom, USA

The U.S. Navy had adopted a "crew"-necked, short-sleeved, white cotton un-
dershirt to be worn under sailors' V-necked uniforms as early as 1913, for the
purpose of covering their chests. But the history of the T-shirt, so named in
allusion to the shape it takes when it is laid out flat, seems to have begun during World War I, when American troops noticed European soldiers wearing
lightweight cotton undershirts during the hot and humid European summer
days. Compared to the wool uniforms that the American soldiers wore, these
undershirts were far more comfortable, and they quickly caught on with the
troops. By World War II, both the navy and the army had included the
T-shirt as standard-issue underwear. "T-shirt" soon became an official word
in American English, and the big screen contributed to its increase in popularity. In 1951, audiences of *A Streetcar Named Desire* were shocked and
thrilled to see Marlon Brando's T-shirt ripped off his body, revealing his naked
chest. By 1955, the T-shirt, once underwear, had become outerwear.

Henry F. Phillips, American, 1890–1958
Phillips Head Screw, early 1930s
Steel
Manufacturer: Phillips Screw Company, USA

Noticing a need for more precise fasteners, especially for screws with better torque and better handling, Henry Phillips of Portland, Oregon, set out to design a screw that could be rotated by imposing on its center with an automated screwdriver. That is how the cross-shaped incision on the screw head was born. The screw was also easier to center and therefore more suitable to a mechanized production line, a feat that Phillips could prove in 1936, when his invention was applied to the line manufacturing Cadillacs at General Motors. Phillips, under siege for almost twenty years, lost his patent to his innumerable imitators in 1949, but—some consolation—his name lives on with every brand and manufacturer.

Maurice Levy, American, n.d.
Lipstick Tube, 1915
This model manufactured by Guerlain, France

While lipstick has been used for thousands of years, on both men and women to varying degrees of popularity, the archetype of the tube we come to recognize as an iconic marker of the consummate lady was invented only in 1915.

A stint of puritanical ideals stifled lipstick wearers in North America until the beginning of the twentieth century, when French cosmetics company Guerlain first put lip coloring onto a stick. In 1912, marching suffragettes like Elizabeth Cady Stanton and Charlotte Perkins Gilman wore lipstick as a sign of emancipation from ruling men. The teens were the grand moment in cosmetics packaging progress, with the introduction of Maybelline mascara, Max Factor pancake, and, in 1915, the lipstick tube. Maurice Levy, working within the Scovil Manufacturing Company of Waterbury, Connecticut, developed a revolutionary bullet-shaped metal case for lipstick. The affordable Scovil metal tube helped popularize the product across classes and throughout World War I and the Depression era. The first tubes did not yet have the threaded inner mechanism to push the lipstick up with its progressive use. The tube design's later developments inspired a scientist at Henkel, the German chemical products giant, to design the Pritt glue stick in 1969.

George Grant Blaisdell, American, 1895–1978
Zippo Lighter, 1932
Chrome
Manufacturer: Zippo Manufacturing Company, USA

A matter of pride for American design, the indefatigable Zippo was based on an Austrian scheme for a windproof lighter, adapted and given life to by George Blaisdell of Bradford, Pennsylvania, where the factory is still based today.

While the first prototype—with an external hinge on the cap—was introduced in 1932, the 1936 patent refers to the definitive model with the elegant, if boxy, flush body. The name Zippo, based on "zipper," soon became famous around the world and ignited collecting frenzies and unrequited passion. With only a few minor tweaks to the production line, the Zippo is still made today the way it was in the 1930s.

ACKNOWLEDGMENTS

As we all should know, ideas, even great ideas, are three dollars a pound. The real challenge is making them happen, and that is a feat one can hardly ever accomplish alone. This is my favorite task, celebrating those who pushed me out of my thoughts and into action.

The Museum of Modern Art is my life, my luck, and my inspiration. Humble Masterpieces started as an exhibition there, in our Queens location, in the summer of 2004. My first bow of gratitude goes thus to all of MoMA and in particular to the people who were instrumental in making this show happen, from Terry Riley, the Philip Johnson Chief Curator of Architecture and Design, whose unwavering support is behind all my curatorial accomplishments, to Jerry Neuner, who designed the disarmingly warm and clear installation, to James Kuo and Burns Magruder, who devised the bold graphic image for the show. And then there are many others, the whole museum as a matter of fact, but one gigantic acknowledgment in particular goes to Patricia Juncosa Vecchierini, an intern at that time and now a curatorial assistant, who contributed so much to the whole project and without whom this and other exhibitions would never be as good and meaningful.

The exhibition at MoMA featured about 120 objects, but fewer than fifty of them appear in this book. First of all, we had to make sure that all the objects presented here were available today, in an affordable store somewhere in the world, while the selection in the exhibition featured many discontinued, albeit gorgeous, objects from the MoMA collection. Moreover, the "suggestions" books in the MoMA gallery in 2004 filled very rapidly with great ideas that I could not resist. I thus thank the MoMA public for their great recommendations and their enthusiasm.

And now, the book. It all began with Melik Kaylan. Through Melik, who is a human lighter, of great discussions, sometimes of worthy controversies, often of interesting consequences, I met Judith Regan. Or better, my husband Larry (Carty) and I met Judith. Larry and Judith are two of the most energetic, fast-talking, passionate, and enthusiastic people I know. Just watching them talk about the weather would be enough of an inspiration for anybody to spring into action. Imagine having them focus on *your* ideas and what *you* want to do, first solo, then in tandem. Dear readers, I had no choice. Seriously speaking, I wish everybody a companion like Larry, whose goal is to help me achieve whatever I set my mind and heart on, and a friend like Judith, who first of all believed in the ideas I always thought were too quirky to happen, and who showed me you can be an indomitable force in the professional world without ever sacrificing your playfulness, instinct, and feelings.

I thank with all my heart Cassie Jones, who edited this book, taught me all the ropes, and always showed patience. Eva Hagberg not only helped me with the research, but also wrote a great part of the texts that describe the objects in detail. It is not what she had initially signed for. I want her to know that this passion and generosity are what will make her great at any endeavor. Many thanks also to Aliza Fogelson, who helped me iron out the initial details.

It was wonderful to work with Richard Ljoenes, who art directed *Humble Masterpieces*. It was out first collaboration, I hope the first of many. Photographer Francesco Mosto lived inside his macro lens for many weeks and lovingly showed me new details of the objects that I thought I was already familiar with. And Tammi Guthrie, in Cassie Jones's office, was ever so graceful and sunny, even when she was soliciting my belated notes.

I also would like to thank designers, engineers, and architects from all over the world for giving me endless pain and delight with their work.

CHRONOLOGICAL INDEX

Frisbee. Walter Frederick Morrison and Warren Franscioni, 1948. *112–13*

Flip-Flops. Unknown designer, late 1940s. *176–77*

Bar Code. Norman Joseph Woodland and Bernard "Bob" Silver, ca. 1948. *46–47*

Double-Chambered Tea Bag. Adolf Rambold, 1949. *62–63*

Soft Contact Lenses. Otto Wichterle, 1950s. *164–65*

Bic Cristal. Décolletage Plastique Design Team, 1950. *68–69*

Ping-Pong Paddle. Horoi Satoh, 1952. *134–35*

Wiffle Ball. David N. and David A. Mullany, 1953. *168–69*

Lamello Biscuit Joiner. Hermann Steiner, 1955. *138–39*

LEGO Building Bricks. Godtfred Kirk Christiansen, 1954–58. *180–81*

Chupa Chups Lollipop. Enric Bernat i Fontlladosa, 1958. *120–21*

Tetra Brik. Tetra Pak Research Laboratories, 1959. *132–33*

Bubble Wrap. Marc A. Chavannes and Alfred W. Fielding, 1960. *16–17*

Duracell AA Battery. Duracell (company design), 1960. *124–25*

Super Ball. Norman Stingley, 1965. *66–67*

O Series Scissors. Olof Bäckström, 1960. *194–95*

Mascara Wand. Unknown designer, 1960s. *188–89*

Kikkoman Soy Sauce Dispenser. Kenji Ekuan and GK Design Group, 1961. *98–99*

Light-Emitting Diode (LED). Nick Holonyak, 1962. *156–57*

Boxes. Gene Hurwitt, ca. 1965. *64–65*

SwissChamp Knife. Karl Elsener, ca. 1968. *6–7*

Spoon Straw. Arthur A. Aykanian, 1968. *32–33*

Digital Compact Disc. Philips and Sony Research Laboratories, 1970s. *186–87*

E-A-R Earplug. Ross Gardner, 1972. *80–81*

J1 Bic Disposable Lighter. Flaminaire (company design), 1972. *166–67*

Rubik's Cube. Ernö Rubik, 1974. *148–49*

Beverage Can with Non-removable Pull-Tab. Daniel F. Cudzik, 1975. *154–55*

I ❤ NY Logo. Milton Glaser, 1976. *56–57*

Jelly Belly Jelly Beans. Herman Goelitz Rowland, 1976. *44–45*

Post-it Note. Art Fry and Spencer Silver, ca. 1977. *76–77*

Filofax Ring-Bound Organizer. Norman & Hill, now Filofax, late 1970s. *60–61*

Screwpull Corkscrew. Herbert Allen, 1979. *22–23*

#1 Slant Tweezer. Tweezerman (company design), ca. 1980. *48–49*

Swatch Wristwatch. Swatch (company design), 1983. *18–19*

AWS-1 Hex Wrench Set. Howard and Eric Hawkins, 1984. *162–63*

Solo Traveler Coffee-Cup Lid. Jack Clements, 1986. *72–73*

Mini Maglite. Anthony Maglica, 1987. *172–73*

Good Grips Paring Knife. Smart Design, 1989. *136–37*

International Symbol of HIV and AIDS Awareness. Visual AIDS Artists Caucus, 1991. *90–91*

Flashcard. Iain Sinclair, 1992. *74–75*

VarioPac Trigger Jewel Cases. Klaus Gloger, 1992. *140–41*

Stapleless Stapler. Walter Windisch, ca. 1993. *116–17*

Java Jacket Coffee-Cup Sleeve. Jay Sorensen, 1993. *50–51*

X-Band Rubber Bands. Unknown designer, 1995. *128–29*

Transforming Sphere. Chuck Hoberman, 1995. *190–91*

Cable Turtle. Flex Development BV, 1996. *28–29*

Moscardino Disposable Spoon/Fork. Giulio Iacchetti and Matteo Ragni, 2000. *54–55*

Kadokeshi Plastic Eraser. Hideo Kanbara, 2001. *84–85*

Stainless Steel Soap. Unknown designer, 2001. *36–37*

Band-Aid Advanced Healing Blister. Coloplast (company design), 2002. *100–101*